Mountain Climbing
for Beginners

By the same author

COMMANDO CLIMBER

HIGH ARCTIC

RAKAPOSHI

SNOW COMMANDO

GREENLAND

Mountain Climbing for Beginners

Mike Banks

with drawings by
Toby Buchan

Edited by Andy Kauffman

Stein and Day/*Publishers*/New York

First published in the United States of America in 1978.

Copyright © 1977 by Mike Banks
Copyright © 1978 by Stein and Day, Inc.

Printed in the United States of America.
Stein and Day/*Publishers*/Scarborough House,
Briarcliff Manor, N.Y. 10510

Library of Congress Cataloging in Publication Data

Banks, Mike, 1922-
    Mountain climbing for beginners.

    Includes index.
    1. Mountaineering.   I.   Kauffman, Andrew John.
II. Title.
GV200.B36   1978   796.5'22   77-17607
ISBN 0-8128-2448-2
ISBN 0-8128-2447-4 pbk.

Contents

Illustrations

Acknowledgments

I am greatly indebted to two of my climbing companions, Richard Brooke and Robert Moulton, for their most valuable and expert help and advice.

Cover photograph of rock climbing in the Dolomites by Mike Banks.

Mountain Climbing
for Beginners

Chapter 1

Why do it?

Mountaineering is a highly rewarding but potentially dangerous activity. The beginner must therefore start cautiously, learning the safety measures, selecting the correct equipment and then practising the many and varied climbing skills under expert guidance. The aim of this book is to help the young mountaineer identify the host of practical problems which must be mastered before the sport can be enjoyed in safety.

The fundamentals of mountaineering, with emphasis on safety aspects, are fully covered. Rock climbing technique, which is the basis of the sport, is described in detail. However, in order to present a balanced picture of mountaineering, an outline is also given of the craft of snow and ice climbing and the way in which the harder rock climbs, using artificial aids, are tackled.

Mountaineering presents challenge and adventure. Young people usually take it up on their own initiative to meet some vaguely defined but strongly felt need.

People take their first step in mountaineering in many different ways. Lord Hunt, the Mount Everest expedition leader, was given a climbing book as a Christmas present when he was a boy which so fired his imagination that he decided to give climbing a try. He is now in his seventies and still an active mountaineer! Others may start as walkers who become ambitious and try a hike in the hills where, for the first time, they come under the strong spell of the mountain atmosphere. They may see the climbers setting off from the valleys with their ropes and special equipment; they may see them in action on the rock faces and feel irresistibly drawn towards what is obviously an exciting, even if possibly a rather frightening, sport.

Others may get their first glimpse of the mountain scene by taking part in a group visit to the hills often organized by their school as an official outdoor pursuits activity. Organizations such as the Boy Scouts of America or Outward Bound movements run introductory courses in mountain activities. For students undergoing further education, a start may be made by attending a beginners' meet arranged by the university mountaineering club. Outside the educational system it is usual to find, in many big cities, a climbing club which will welcome and help beginners. Finally, in some popular climbing areas there are professional guides and climbing schools, but they require payment, and in the United States their quality and reliability are not uniform. None of these organizations push youngsters into mountaineering as they are impelled into organized sport at school. They simply lead volunteers to the threshold. It is then up to them if they decide, of their own free will, to step across that threshold and turn themselves into climbers.

The lucky ones start climbing by being taken out by an experienced friend and this is an excellent way of learning, always provided that the 'instructor' is himself well trained and has the knack of passing on his knowledge.

The first impulse that prompts a person to climb is as unpredictable as human nature itself. Some will want to test themselves in what they imagine to be a dangerous situation, to experience a thrill on a steep rock face. Others may take up climbing as a healthy, non-competitive sport, to be enjoyed with pleasant, like-minded companions out in the fresh mountain air. Others, and I suspect the fourteen-year-old John Hunt was one of them, feel a sense of wonderment in the immensity and grandeur of the mountain world. Some instinct tells them that the hills will enrich them spiritually as well as offering a challenging sport.

Whatever reason first prompts a young person to go to the hills, from a dare-devil search for a thrill to a quest for something deeper in life, the realities of the situation soon dominate: the right equipment must be procured; a journey must be made to the mountain range; once in the hills the problems of weather, mountain navigation and, ultimately, overcoming the difficulties of climbing steep rock, extend the mind and body to their full limit.

The History of Mountaineering

It is interesting to trace how mountaineering developed as a sport. It evolved from mountain travel. In the eighteenth and early nineteenth century geographers and scientists became interested in the mountain regions and needed to penetrate their recesses and ascend their heights to gain knowledge. They invariably hired local guides, the most famous of whom were in the Alps, who were skilled mountain travellers and accustomed to moving over very steep mountainsides.

Some of these early scientists and travellers found that over and above their scientific interest there was a tremendous fascination in the mountain world. Particularly after Mont Blanc (15,771 ft; 4807 m), the highest mountain in the Alps, was ascended by a Frenchman, Dr Paccard, in 1786, mountaineering became established as a sport in its own right without any pretence to scientific investigation. Climbers began to vie with each other to pick off the unclimbed summits of the Alps, the British predominating. This phase closed with the dramatic ascent of the Matterhorn by Edward Whymper in 1865, just ahead of an Italian party on the other side of the mountain. Four of Whymper's rope of seven fell to their death on the descent.

With all the major summits climbed, mountaineers began to climb peaks by hitherto unclimbed flanks or ridges so that, for instance, all four ridges of the pyramidal-shaped Matterhorn were eventually climbed. This process of filling in the detail continued, and still continues to the present day, so that most major peaks now have many different routes recorded on them. The first climbers took the easiest way up and managed with very simple equipment. The rope was used principally by the guide to give his client a good heave at the right moment. By the end of the nineteenth century the sport and the equipment had become far more sophisticated.

The rope was used to secure one man to the rock while the other climbed and an ice axe had replaced the long pole, or alpenstock, and was used to cut steps up hitherto unclimbable snow or ice slopes.

The sport accelerated in the twentieth century. In place of crude hobnails on the boots, specially made nails with sharp teeth, called *tricounis*, were used to give a better grip on the rock. Ice claws, called *crampons*, were strapped onto the boots and enabled climbers to move fast and safely on ice or hard snow without having to waste time and effort in cutting steps.

Because the climbing season in the Alps was restricted to the summer, mountaineers sought ways of enjoying their sport during the remainder of the year. In this way rock climbing on lower hills evolved as a sport in its own right. The development in Britain was in many ways typical.

Climbers went to the hills to keep in practice for the Alps and found that rock climbing on the crags was a most satisfying experience. They first ascended the gullies, especially in winter when they were filled with snow and gave good training in alpine techniques. The rocks were climbed in all seasons. After the gullies attention was paid to the ridges and buttresses, the routes becoming steeper and more open as the century progressed. Finally, the sheer, smooth walls were climbed. By this time the standard of difficulty was such that the harder climbs could not be done in tricouni-nailed boots. Rubber-soled tennis or gym shoes were necessary. By World War I rock climbing techniques had been refined and developed very much into the form we use today. Indeed, by 1914 the American Oliver Perry-Smith had made ascents among the spires of Germany's Saxon "Little Switzerland" which still rank among the hardest climbs in the district.

However, as in every other sport, standards are relentlessly being forced upwards, greatly helped by improvements in safety equipment. The beginner of today is soon doing climbs which, even a generation ago, would have been considered to be only within the ability of the top climbers.

Mountaineering in its ultimate form is the expedition to an unclimbed mountain in a remote range. Exploration of the far-off mountains gathered momentum early in the twentieth century when the Alps had become thoroughly explored. Climbers turned their attention first of all to the Himalayas and the Andes, and then to the remotest ranges of the world until today most of the great peaks even in the Arctic and Antarctic have been climbed. There are still, however, mountains beyond number which are awaiting a first ascent, but they tend to be peaks of the second magnitude in the most inaccessible regions. So the scope is still there!

*   *   *   *   *

The remainder of this book is devoted to the nuts and bolts of mountaineering. Important though these technicalities may be, try to keep in sight the end product—the enjoyment of mountaineering. It is a pursuit which may merely remain a satisfying form of recreation although it can easily develop into a passion. It can provide pleasant and healthy exercise or it may take the climber to the full stretch of his utmost mental and physical capacity. It may lead the mountaineer into the pleasant countryside of his homeland hills or it may lure him to the unclimbed ranges in the remote and wild places of the earth.

Chapter 2

Hill Walking

Hill walking is a basic mountaineering skill and may be defined as travel in the mountains which does not require the specialized techniques, principally the use of the rope, used in rock climbing or snow and ice climbing. Because rock climbing crags are often deep in the heart of the mountains, frequently high up on the hillsides, the typical mountaineer may spend more time hill walking than he does actually climbing.

When out hill walking a very careful watch must be kept on the weather. It must be realized that, even on the apparently mildest day, cloud can suddenly descend, blotting out the landscape, and a high wind with chilling rain may occur at the same time. Even at the height of summer these conditions could be potentially fatal to an inexperienced and ill-equipped party. If their navigation is bad they may blunder onto dangerously steep ground where it is only too easy for a tired, wet, cold and demoralized young climber to become careless and fall to his or her death. If an ill-equipped party decides to stay put, and face a night of storm on a high mountain, the heat loss from the body through thin, wet clothing can easily lead to a condition called exposure* which is one of the most common reasons for death in the mountains. The moral is clear: the would-be mountaineer must, as a matter of the utmost priority, ensure that he is correctly equipped and properly trained in the skills of hill walking. It is of paramount importance that he is able to navigate confidently with map and compass over steep ground in very bad visibility or at night.

It is an unforgettable experience to be caught in a severe storm in the mountains. The whole world, which a short time before was pleasant and

*In climber's jargon 'exposure' is also used to indicate that there is a sheer drop below a certain piece of rock. A climb up a vertical wall would be described as 'exposed'.

reasonable, is brutally transformed. The lashing rain or sleet makes it difficult to look upwind, the buffeting of the wind can blow you off your feet and you can feel the warmth literally being sucked out of any exposed flesh. It is difficult to hold a map and to concentrate calmly on accurate navigation. An inexperienced or badly led party can quite easily be induced by the ferocity of the storm into making hasty decisions. There is then a temptation to grasp what seem to be the quick and easy ways out of trouble, an ill-considered short-cut, for instance, instead of working out carefully what is the correct navigational solution. An experienced mountaineer can even, in a strange sort of way, enjoy getting the better of a storm. There is a dour satisfaction in battling against the power of nature and it is a rare moment when careful navigation pays off and the expected landmark looms out of the cloud ahead to confirm that you are on course.

Many people regard hill walking as an end in itself and there are undoubtedly far more hill walkers than rock climbers. They simply enjoy mountain walking and leave it at that. They are not attracted by rock climbing which they probably regard as an unjustifiable risk. The dedicated mountaineer on the other hand wants to enjoy the total mountain experience. Certainly he enjoys his hill walking but he also wants to traverse the hills when they are deep in snow and he also wants to follow the finest and most spectacular routes to the summits—and that often involves rock climbing.

There is a twilight zone between hill walking and climbing called 'scrambling', which indicates that the use of the hands is required to surmount a rock obstacle but that the climbing rope is unnecessary. The trouble about scrambling is that it can mean different things to different people. As an extreme example the famous Victorian mountaineer, Whymper, published a best-seller called *Scrambles among the Alps* in which he described a number of the hardest climbs of the times, including his first ascent of the Matterhorn. Some scrambles! A really talented climber will scramble easily and safely over quite difficult rock, with a lethal drop below him, where an inexperienced person would need to use the rope and would justifiably regard the route as a climb and not a scramble. For our purposes we will include under the heading of hill walking only those scrambles where the rock is very easy and is not poised over a drop where a fall would result in a dangerous accident.

Clothing and Equipment

Because the clothing and equipment used in hill walking has to stand up under extreme conditions, it must be robust and of proven design and quality. Second rate or make-do gear must be firmly discarded. The following items are required by the hill walker:

Boots. It is most important to procure a pair of really robust and comfortable mountain boots. The sole should be of composition rubber, usually called vibram. The uppers should be of good quality leather. For purely hill walking purposes, it is best to have a supple, flexible sole. However, if the ultimate object is to graduate to rock climbing, the sole should be stiffer, thus enabling the climber to stand more comfortably on small toe-holds as will be explained in the next chapter. The boots should be fitted over two pairs of thick woollen socks and should be roomy enough for the toes to be wiggled freely. If the toes are tightly pressed together, the circulation is restricted and cold feet will result. Finally, take your time in finding a really comfortable pair of boots and do not be rushed by a pressurizing salesman. If you buy hastily you will repent at leisure with blisters and sore ankles. Once you have bought the boots, break them in slowly and keep the leather well treated with a water-proofing polish and the occasional application of a softening agent. When they get wet, never dry them rapidly in front of a fire. This will harm the leather.

Stockings. It is usual to wear one pair of knee-length stockings and one pair of shorter socks. Not only are two pairs necessary in cold weather but they also pad the feet more effectively.

Knickers. Mountaineers prefer knickers rather than trousers because they allow freer leg movement when making high steps. With ordinary trousers there is considerable drag at the knee, particularly when they are wet. Knickers should be of a thick weave, to make them relatively wind proof, and have plenty of wool in them for warmth.

Undergarments. Warm underpants and a string or thermal vest are recommended, together with a thick shirt with a long tail so that it does not work up from the trousers. A good, thick woollen roll neck sweater must also be carried.

Windproof parka. Modern inventiveness has been unable to produce a cloth that will keep out heavy rain and at the same time allow the considerable amount of water vapour, or sweat, to escape from the body through the clothing during hard exertion, such as walking uphill. If it is raining the hill walker has the choice of getting wet from the outside with the rain or putting on a waterproof jacket and getting wet from the inside with sweat. Usually the latter is preferred. It is advisable to carry a lightweight windproof jacket or parka, which will keep the wind out and therefore keep the body warm. This garment should be of a fabric that 'breathes' and therefore lets the sweat out. The windproof parka might be showerproof but it will not keep out heavy and persistent rain, particularly after it has become worn. Probably the best, and one of the most expensive breathing cloths, is called 'ventile'. My own preference is for a cheap, light windproof which only keeps the wind out.

Waterproof garments. The hills are rainy and it is vitally important to keep dry in order to avert the danger of exposure caused by rapid heat loss through wet clothing. A long outer jacket, called a *cagoule*, is a necessity. Cagoules are normally made of nylon treated with neoprene or polyurethane to make them waterproof. They have a hood which can be tightened round the neck, and elasticated cuffs to keep water from running up the arms. The legs are kept dry by waterproof trousers of the same material. This waterproof covering can greatly reduce hardship through cold or even save a mountaineer's life if he is overtaken by night, benighted as we say, or caught in a storm.

Headwear. A woollen balaclava helmet is best but any warm hat that protects the ears and back of the neck is suitable.

Gloves. Fingered gloves are not recommended except in mild weather. In cold conditions mitts should be worn. They have a separate thumb compartment but the fingers are not separated into different compartments. The best are called Dachsteins and are made of very thick, almost windproof, pre-shrunk wool. Lightweight waterproof nylon over-mitts should be worn in very wet or windy conditions.

Down jacket. This is an expensive but very pleasant optional extra. The French name *duvet* is often used to describe a long-sleeved, down-filled jacket. It is very light and immensely warm. It is pleasant to wear during, say, a longish lunch break on a cold day, or around camp in winter. It can be a life saver if benighted in winter but there is one snag: down loses most of its insulating quality if it becomes wet. Great care must therefore be taken to keep the garment dry. As an alternative to down, some jackets use a filling of non-absorbent artificial fibre which remains effective when wet. They also tend to be cheaper.

Rucksack. A very wide range of rucksacks is available to meet specialized needs. The rock climber will prefer a light rucksack with no side pockets so that it does not catch on the rock. The hill walker out for the day will prefer a light rucksack with some outside pockets. If a camp is to be made, and a tent, sleeping bag, cooking gear and food is to be carried, a frame rucksack is necessary for weights of about 40 lbs or over.

All the clothing and equipment described above, with the exception of the down jacket which is optional, should be procured by the beginner. In addition he should obtain the following small items of **personal safety equipment** which should be kept permanently in the flap pocket of the rucksack:

> Whistle—one with a shrill note.
> Compass—Silva type or similar.
> Small first aid kit—with plasters for blisters.
> Torch—the type with a headlamp is best.
> Pencil and paper in a polythene bag.

Before you set off

Careful planning and thorough preparation will go a long way to ensure the success and enjoyment of a mountain walk; neglect of these will probably lead to frustration, perhaps to discomfort or even to a tragic and totally unnecessary accident.

The size and strength of the party must now be considered. Obviously at least one person must be well experienced and assume the leadership. The absolute minimum is two persons but three or four is better. In the event of a mishap to a party of four, one person can stay with the casualty while two go down to the valley for help. There is obviously an upper limit. A very large party gets strung out over the hillside and is difficult to control. It also causes unwelcome delays. Ten is the reasonable upper limit per leader. A small group of experienced hill walkers will not need a formal leader.

Having settled the size of the party the next thing to do is to plan the route. Guide books are always available in popular areas which will recommend the best walks and possibly contain useful route descriptions.

The route must now be worked out on the map. The total distance to be travelled and the gain in height should be calculated and related to the stamina of the party. In the mountains it is more appropriate to measure a journey in hours rather than miles. Here 'Naismith's Rule' may be used as a rough guide. This rule applies to lightly laden, fit adults moving over easy terrain. It allows three miles in the hour plus half an hour for every one thousand feet of ascent. It does not allow for the mountaineer becoming fatigued, neither does it allow for bad weather. Particularly with young persons, the rule will become progressively over-optimistic as the day wears on, if the weather worsens, or if the ground is very rough.

Having concluded that the route is within the time available and the ability of the party, a route card should be made out, using the following headings:

From   To   Distance   Bearing   Height   Estimated Time

It is also useful to look at the route carefully through a magnifying glass which concentrates the attention on all the details and might reveal snags that are easily overlooked at a more sweeping glance. Difficulties should be anticipated and a number of escape routes should be selected. Then, if the weather breaks or if a member of the party becomes over-tired, it is an immense relief to follow a pre-planned escape route rather than try to work one out under adverse conditions.

A note giving full details of the proposed route together with an estimated time of return should be left with a responsible person, such as a Forest Service Ranger, who will then take any necessary action if the party is seriously overdue. Alternatively, the note may be left in the tent, if camping, or behind the windshield wiper of the party's car. The leader should also note the location and telephone number of the nearest mountain rescue post. Shortly prior to departure he should get the latest weather report and, if bad weather is forecast, he should be prepared either to alter his plan, possibly keeping to a lower altitude, or to beat a hasty retreat.

The last thing to do before setting off is to check the contents of rucksacks. The clothing already described should be worn or carried, according to the weather conditions, and the personal safety equipment should be in the flap pocket of the rucksack. In addition each person must carry a lunch meal, usually sandwiches, chocolate and some fruit. Extra emergency rations of high food value should be added and also some spare clothing, particularly socks and a sweater, which should be kept dry in polythene.

The leader must carry a map, some hand flares and a climbing rope. He should also ensure that a sleeping bag and a large waterproof nylon or polythene bag big enough for a man to get into, called a survival bag, are carried in the party. These could give life saving protection against the wet and cold in the event of a serious accident.

Out on the Hills

An early start is one of the best ways of ensuring a successful day's walk or climb. Then, if things do not go according to plan—and often they do not—time is probably available to put them right.

Once on your way, no matter how fit and energetic individuals may feel, a slow mountain pace should be set. This has been described as 'the easy stride of the hills' and is the ambling pace that shepherds or mountain guides set. It might look leisurely but it is the sort of pace that you can keep hour after hour without becoming out of breath or badly overheated. The wisdom of generations of hill folk has gone into that easy, rhythmic, but somewhat relentless pace.

The leader should be constantly scanning the ground ahead to select the easiest route and check his progress against the map and watch. Often he will be following a mountain trail which is marked with small heaps of stones called cairns. The party should keep together and the speed of the leader adjusted to that of the slowest member. The party should never be split or strung out over the mountainside. It is quite usual, after a chilly start, to warm up on the first good slope. A short halt should be made to take off any unnecessary clothing. Some people sweat more profusely than others and can suffer from serious overheating, which reduces body efficiency, while others remain unaffected. Also, of course, sweating will dampen clothing and badly impair its insulation.

Sometimes obstacles, such as a rocky step, may be unavoidable. The leader must recognize that they cause delay. He should not therefore press on directly he has crossed the obstacle because this will string the party out. He should wait until the last member is across; then all go on together.

If a stone is dislodged, it can gather speed and become very dangerous. In the first place, do your utmost never to dislodge a stone. If a stone begins to fall, give a loud shout of "Rock!" If on hearing this shout, you see the stone bouncing down slowly towards you, it can be dodged. If it is whizzing down a steep rock wall, either dive for cover or, if there is none, quickly put your rucksack over your head to gain at least partial protection.

The leader must have eyes everywhere. In addition to selecting the route he must keep a careful watch on the party, particularly when some of the members are young. If it becomes apparent that the route is too ambitious he will have to make the sometimes difficult decision of either turning back or shortening the route. He must also keep a sharp watch on the weather and become alert if, for instance, little wisps of cloud begin to form around the summits or if the cloud ceiling begins to descend and obscure the tops. He must also be watchful for squalls which might quickly sweep up a valley and drench the party. Even though it might be a disappointment to the stronger members, the leader must unhesitatingly take the decision to turn back if he thinks the party, or any individual member, might be running into danger.

Walking uphill is very heavy exercise. Plenty of good food should be taken—and eaten. If the party begins to flag, perhaps in unpleasant weather, a meal can work wonders in restoring warmth and energy. It is also important not to suffer from thirst. It is usually safe to drink from mountain streams if it is obvious that there are no habitations upstream. Some mountaineers carry a short length of plastic tube through which they can suck water from shallow pools which can often be found even on otherwise waterless mountainsides or ridges.

Extra careful attention must be given to the descent because this is when the party is tired and therefore most accident-prone. If the descent is made according to plan down a known and well-marked track, there should be no problems. However, it sometimes happens that an unplanned descent has to be made, perhaps retreating before the onset of night or bad weather. The golden rule is not to undertake a particular descent route unless you can see clear to the valley and can observe that the route is safe *the whole way down*. It is potentially dangerous to descend a convex slope—one that steepens and plunges down out of sight. There might be unclimbable cliffs lurking out of sight which would require an already tired party to retrace its steps uphill. Neither is it a good idea to follow a watercourse. A stream might seem to lead invitingly downhill in exactly the right direction but it may turn into a waterfall that cannot be climbed down. In any case water tends to follow the shortest, as opposed to the easiest, route downhill.

In winter the hills are usually covered with snow and ice. Hill walking in these conditions requires special equipment and skills which are described in Chapter 7.

Finally, it is very important that mountaineers should observe both the country code and sensible rules of conservation. There is no one to collect the garbage left on the hills and a popular summit can quickly become a mountain slum if climbers fail to take their lunch left-overs back to the valley.

As more and more young people take to the hills, a serious erosion problem can occur, especially on very popular hill walks in National

Parks. The thin layer of top soil on the mountainside can quite quickly get eroded away. The responsible mountaineer must therefore co-operate with the conservation authorities and, for instance, observe diversion notices where an overworn section of path is being given a chance to recover.

Mountain Navigation

The mountaineer frequently has to move through cloud and sometimes may have to travel at night. He may well have to steer a route which avoids dangerous cliff faces and the safety of the party will depend utterly on good, confident mountain navigation. Every person who goes into the hills must know how to use the map and compass in mountain conditions against the time when it might be necessary, for instance, to descend quickly to the valley to summon help.

This is not a text-book of map reading. However, the aspiring mountaineer, if not already a skilled map reader, should most certainly read such a text-book to understand the rudiments of map reading such as the difference between magnetic, grid and true north; and the use of grid references which can be vital in an emergency.

It is best to use a map with a scale of 1:25,000, or about $2\frac{1}{4}$ inches to the mile, in the mountains. The large scale makes it easier to read and gives plenty of detail, especially the line of walls or hedges which are absent from the smaller scale maps. These can be very helpful in mountain navigation in bad visibility. Maps with a scale of 1:50,000 and 1-inch to 1-mile are also suitable.

From the outset an effort should be made to improve your ability at mountain map reading. Assuming a reasonable familiarity with the subject in the valley, the first thing to do is to get the feel by relating the unfamiliar mountain landscape to the map. Great attention must be concentrated on contour lines which are the key to mountain map reading. Features such as ridges, buttresses or shallow scoops in the mountainside should be observed closely and then identified on the map. Conversely, the contours should be studied and where, for instance, there is a 'wiggle' going up a mountainside, it should be identified as a spur or a depression. Most important, the steepness of a slope as observed by eye must be related to the closeness together of the contour lines. It will then be possible to assess the steepness of a slope from the map and to judge whether it would be safe to venture on to. Study very closely how rock faces are

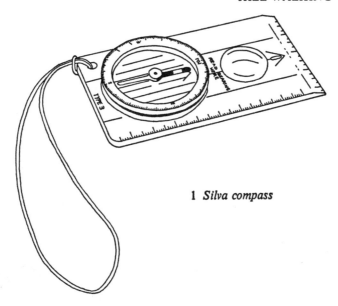

1 *Silva compass*

marked, because quite soon you will either want to find them to climb them or avoid them to find a safe, quick route.

The compass is essential in the hills. Without doubt the best is the Silva model, a Swedish invention. It is light, accurate and made of transparent plastic. The important thing to remember is that it is two separate instruments in one—a compass and a protractor. The compass, of course, is used to steer a course or take a bearing *on the ground*. The plastic body, in conjunction with the rotating centrepiece, is used as a protractor to give a very quick and easy means of taking a bearing between two points *from the map*.

The following should be practised until they become second nature:

Taking a grid bearing between two points from the map.
Converting the grid bearing to a magnetic bearing.
Taking a magnetic bearing onto a point on the ground.
Converting the magnetic bearing to a grid bearing and marking it on the map.

In other words this takes information from the map and transfers it to the ground, and vice-versa—and that is what map reading is all about.

In clear weather you should always be able to find your position, and therefore work out your route, by a careful comparison of map and ground. It might even be necessary to take a couple of bearings on prominent features to establish your exact position.

The real test of navigation comes in bad visibility or at night. Clouds often swirl around the mountains, reducing visibility to a few yards. This should not deter the experienced hill walker. When bad visibility threatens, the navigator should be extra careful to keep check of his position on the map. If he is caught off guard by cloud and finds himself lost in a swirling, white void the best thing to do is to walk back to the last definitely identifiable feature and start afresh from there. Even if there is a track marked on the map it should be remembered that other tracks, including sheep trails or unmarked tracks may criss-cross the marked trail. The compass bearing of the correct trail should be noted and the leader should become immediately suspicious if the party, still apparently following the track, begins to head off in a different direction.

If the mountainside is safe, in other words not too steep and devoid of cliff faces, it is quite in order to navigate down to the valley on a single compass bearing. However, it could well be that a zig-zag route passing between lethal cliffs has to be followed down a ridge. Immense care now has to be taken with the navigation, especially if night is coming on and the party is tired and cold and the navigator therefore prone through mental fatigue to make mathematical mistakes. If a party finds itself lost in such conditions the important thing is to keep together. No matter how strong someone's hunch, they should not be allowed to wander off to check their theory. Having found a positively identified feature, the navigator should proceed very calmly and deliberately marching on his calculated compass bearing. It could well be necessary to check progress by counting the number of paces taken and then to change course at the calculated distance, perhaps to avoid a dangerous point by a safe margin. If visibility is really bad and the route passes close to dangerous cliffs, the party should rope themselves together. In bad visibility, with nothing ahead for the eye to focus on, it is not easy to steer an accurate course walking with the compass held in the hand, trying to keep the compass needle correctly aligned. It is better to get one man to walk ahead so that he can constantly be checked by the navigator with his compass. The navigator will constantly call, 'Go a little right', etc., to keep the man in front on course. He may even have to let the man walk to the limit of visibility and then move him right or left until he is on course, then walk up to him and repeat the process leapfrogging forward. Patience and accuracy are the keynotes and the leader should not be flustered by the impatience of any of his friends. Above all he should put implicit trust in his map and compass and not be lured into letting a friend who 'thinks he knows where he is' lead them off into the cloud.

So much for hill walking. It is possible to start rock climbing on easily accessible crags without bothering to learn how to move safely in the hills, but this would leave a serious gap in the beginner's essential mountaineering knowledge which sooner or later would have to be rectified by anyone wishing to enjoy in safety the freedom of the hills.

Chapter 3

Rock Climbing Equipment

Before we can start rock climbing some extra equipment is required, more specialized than that needed for hill walking. Like everything else, it is expensive these days but the whole range of equipment need not be bought in the first instance. The instructor or experienced leader will bring along most of the special gadgets leaving the beginner merely to provide himself with the correct clothing.

Boots come top of the list. As we discussed, for hill walking the design of the boots is not critical provided that they have composition or vibram soles and are robust, roomy and waterproof. In rock climbing small footholds are often used and highly sophisticated (and, of course, expensive!) boots have been developed. On the other hand, when your life depends on an item, as it will on your boots, then only the best will do.

Climbing boots have corrugated vibram soles and are, of course, tough and waterproof when new. To give a very positive hold, as if your toes were themselves over a small rock hold, the soles are flush with the uppers. In other words there is no protruding welt which, for convenience of manufacture, is common in most footwear. To achieve rigidity, the soles of the boots are stiffened, often by placing a steel plate along the length of the sole. Flexible, sloppy boots give the worrying feeling that they are sliding off a hold, whereas a stiff boot braces the ankle and feels, and indeed is, more secure. This stiffness is also important in snow and ice climbing. The boots should fit comfortably over two pairs of socks and the toes should not be compressed. Climbing boots should be selected with great care—but the price alone will probably ensure that you do this!

For the harder climbs, a more specialized boot is required. The most popular are referred to as **'PAs'** after their inventor, Pierre Alain. They

2 *Climbing boots*

are very light, with canvas or suede uppers and a single, thin, smooth rubber sole. Particularly on dry rock and on sloping holds, they give a superior grip. Some of the hardest climbs are probably impossible without them. PAs should not be purchased until considerable progress has been made in rock climbing.

A protective **helmet**, or 'hard hat', is a must. It performs two functions. It affords considerable protection to the head in the event of a fall and it is a protection against small falling stones. Helmets should always be worn while climbing.

The climber's **rucksack** does not have a frame or outside pockets, which would catch on the rock. It usually has attachments for carrying an ice axe and crampons. The flap should incorporate a zipped pocket.

3 *'PA' boots*

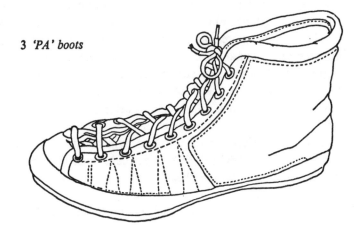

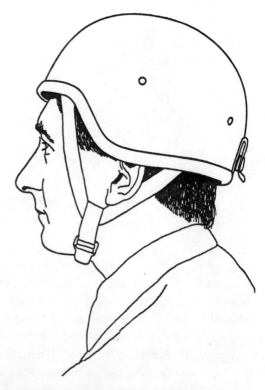

4 *Safety helmet*

Clothing takes a beating during rock climbing and should be both warm and hard wearing. Many climbers prefer knickers to trousers. A thick sweater and a parka complete the outer coverings.

This is a convenient moment to describe the remainder of the rock climber's equipment. The **rope** removes a great deal of the hazard from climbing and reduces the risk to within acceptable limits. Nylon ropes have been developed to embody the very special characteristics required by climbers. They are sold in metric sizes and the standard rope has a diameter of 11 mm and is either 36 m (120 ft approx) or 45 m (150 ft approx) long. They are very strong and have a breaking strain of 4–5000 lbs. They must also stretch up to 40 per cent of their length so as to cushion the effect of a fall. Nylon is flexible to handle, rot proof, and washable. It cannot absorb water and therefore does not get stiff when frozen. The one disadvantage is that nylon melts at the relatively low temperature of 250°C (480°F). Great care must therefore be taken to prevent the rope generating heat, or coming into contact with hot metal, in the event of a fall.

Although very strong, the rope is relatively soft and must be regularly examined for cuts or abrasions. There are two designs of climbing rope. It can be hawser-laid, like most other ropes, where you have three strands twisted together, or *kermantel*, where a central, untwisted, core of nylon fibres is protected by an outside sheath. Both are equally acceptable.

Next comes the problem of attaching the rope to the body. This can be done with a simple bowline or figure-of-eight knot, as will be explained later, or, better, by using a **harness.** The danger of simply tying the rope round the waist is that if the climber is left dangling in the event of a fall, the tight rope round his middle presses against his ribs so that in a matter of minutes he is unable to breathe and will die of suffocation. A harness spreads the load under the thighs, and sometimes also round the shoulders, so that the climber ends up in a more comfortable and safe sitting position. Many designs of harness are available but one which gives support to the thighs is recommended.

If the leader falls, a considerable shock comes onto the rope held by his second man who therefore wears a pair of leather gauntlets, called **belaying gloves,** as a protection against rope burn in this eventuality.

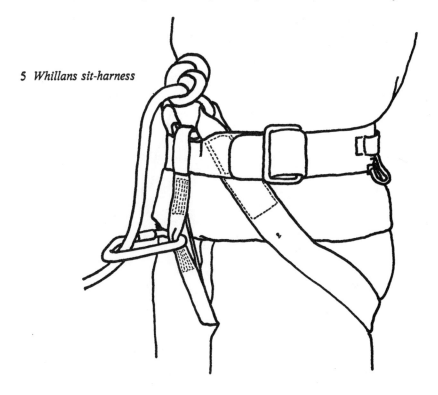

5 *Whillans sit-harness*

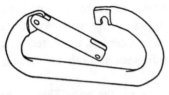

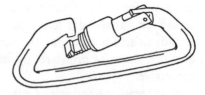

6   *Carabiner*   *Locking carabiner*

To increase the safety of the leader a number of devices enable either the rope or the man to be attached to the rock. They include **slings** or loops of nylon rope or webbing which may be placed round spikes or flakes of rock; **carabiners,** or metal snap links, which enable the sling to be clipped to the climbing rope. Usually this is a simple, oval-shaped, quick-action snap link but a few more elaborate ones are carried which screw securely shut, called locking carabiners. Should the leader fall, a great strain comes on the second man, who is holding the rope, as will be explained later. This strain may be reduced by the use of a friction device called a **Sticht plate** or a **Sticht belay plate.**

There is a whole range of manufactured alloy wedges, called **chocks,** which can be jammed into cracks in the rock. The chocks are either attached to a wire loop or to a nylon sling through which a carabiner is clipped. Finally, if there are no convenient spikes for a

7 *left: Chock on wire sling*
right: Chock on nylon rope sling

8 *Figure-of-eight descender*

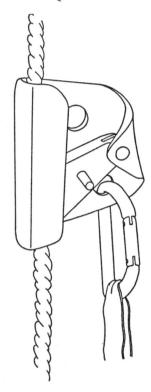

9 *Clog ascender*

sling, or cracks for a chock, a **piton,** or steel blade with a hole at one end, may be driven into the rock with a **piton hammer.** A carabiner is then clipped into the hole at the end of the piton to provide a safe anchor point.

The situation may also arise when a climber wants either to pull himself up or to lower himself down a climbing rope. For the descent **a** metal figure-of-eight device, called a **descender** makes the rope run round some sharp corners which creates friction and absorbs most of the climber's weight. He is then able to pay out the rope and lower himself quite easily. For climbing up **a** rope, less frequently done, a pair of gadgets variously called **ascenders, prusikers** or **jumars** work on a ratchet principle. One at a time they are pushed up the rope where they jam, enabling the climber to ascend in slings dangling from them.

The beginner need only provide himself with suitable clothing, climbing boots and a safety helmet. He should delay purchase of all the other specialized equipment until he has become familiar with its use and can make his purchases with discernment.

Chapter 4

Ropework

The time has now arrived to climb rock, to grapple with the vertical, with nothing but fresh air beneath the soles of our boots! The craft of rock climbing involves the continuous observance of an elaborate framework of safety procedures which mountaineers have evolved to enable them to follow their sport with reasonable safety. There would have been little future for climbing if the result of a slip (and we all have them) was to deposit the climber, probably dead, at the foot of the mountain. The correct use of the climbing rope, together with certain other safety gadgets, greatly minimises the risk if the leader falls. On the other hand, if the second man falls he is seldom in any danger. He is instantly held on the rope from above and merely dangles for a few moments, like a hooked fish.

Everything that follows in this chapter can and must be mastered by anyone learning to climb. We are not here concerned with aptitudes or styles of climbing but with the positive safety methods which are the very foundation of the sport.

Let us follow the progress of a pair of climbers who are walking towards a mountain crag they propose to climb. One is experienced, the other a relative beginner. The leader will probably be carrying a coil of nylon climbing rope slung over his shoulders. It will be 11 mm in diameter, 120 ft or 150 ft in length and neatly coiled. The rope will have been inspected by the leader and coiled in a right-handed direction with loops of a size that hang around the level of his waist and do not dangle around his knees where they catch and are a nuisance. The coils are held together by using one end to make a simple whipping.

Once arrived at the foot of the climb, the rope is completely uncoiled and the two climbers tie on to it. This can be done in a variety of ways,

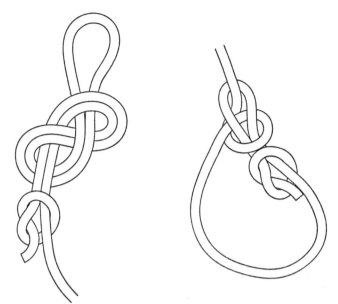

10 *Figure-of-eight knot with stopper knot*   11 *Bowline with stopper knot*

the simplest being a figure-of-eight knot or a bowline, the loop of which is tightened round the waist. Sometimes the rope is threaded through a protective canvas belt which would prevent the nylon rope becoming over-heated and melting if the leader were to fall and his rope bite into the waist of the second man, generating great friction and therefore heat. However, the danger of possible suffocation in the event of a fall when the rope is tied in a single loop round the waist was explained on page 29. A thigh harness is therefore preferred. The climbing rope is connected to the harness by means of a figure-of-eight knot or a bowline and stopper knot or it may be clipped into the harness with a locking carabiner. It will be seen that a sort of chain is being built up. The most important link in the chain is the climbing rope whose breaking

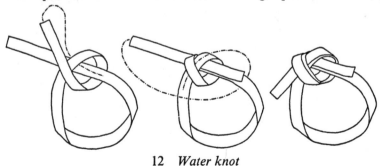

12   *Water knot*

strain will be 4–5000 lbs. When other links are added, for instance the harness, locking carabiner, or any other safety device, care should be taken that a weak link is not inserted or the whole chain may be weakened.

Extra care must be taken when tying knots in nylon rope because they tend to slip before they tighten under shock loading just as a knot tied in a rubber band tends to pull out when tightened. The remedy is to add a stopper knot using the tail of the rope. This is a thumb knot tied round the rope with its tail end. When nylon webbings are tied together, usually to make a sling, a special knot, called a water knot, and no other, must be used. All knots tied in nylon tend to work loose. Therefore, check them frequently and tighten if necessary.

Let us assume that the two climbers are standing on a wide, flat, grassy platform at the foot of their crag and above them rises a slab of rock, well provided with holds, which terminates in a rock ledge 30 ft above. The leader checks that he has all the equipment that he will need and that it is hanging neatly from his waist or round a sling over his shoulder. The second man, whom we will call No 2, pulls on his leather belaying gloves or gauntlets. He stands at the foot of the rock, passes the climbing rope behind his back round his waist and prepares to pay it out as the leader climbs. The part of the rope which goes to the leader is called the active rope; the part still on the ground waiting to be paid out is the inactive end of the rope. No 2 takes an extra twist of the rope round the forearm on the inactive side. This gives him a firmer grip on the rope.

The leader takes a good long look at the rock above him and then starts to climb in a slow, deliberate and rhythmic style, never seeming to hurry or struggle. He reaches the ledge 30 ft up where he stops. These sections of a climb which can be anything from about 15 to 100 ft, are called *pitches*.

At the top of this first pitch the leader has decided to *belay*, or anchor himself to the rock. Luckily at the back of the ledge is a convenient spike of rock. He gives it a good pull to check that it is not loose, then ties himself to it. There are two methods: he can take one of the nylon slings from round his shoulders and drop it over the spike, clipping it into his harness with a locking carabiner. This is the simplest method, provided that his sling is of the right length to hold him tight to the spike. Alternatively he can take the climbing rope, pass it behind the spike, then lead it back to the locking carabiner at his harness, securing it with a figure-of-eight knot. One of the most important things about a belay is to predict where the direction of pull

13 *Leader belayed to a rock spike*

might come on the rope in the event of a fall, and then to ensure that the climber is secured tight to the belay so that the shock of a fall is transferred directly through his body to the strong rock anchor. In this way the shock of holding a fall is greatly reduced. On the other hand if the belay is a sloppy one, with a lot of slack rope between the climber and the anchor, the climber will be hurled off balance when the shock comes on the rope. Not only will he be unable to hold the fall effectively but he may also be injured himself in the process. And two injured climbers is the thing you least want!

The belayer should stand with his back to the rock, facing outwards. The rope or sling holding him to his rock anchor should be tied into his harness in the small of his back. A problem arises with the typical harness where the climbing rope is tied into the front, usually with a locking carabiner. If the belayer connected himself to his anchor from this locking carabiner and the leader fell, he would be twisted violently when the strain came on the rope. The rope might be ripped out of his grasp or he might be injured, or both. The remedy is to ensure that the rope from the anchor is tied into the back of the harness using a separate locking carabiner for this purpose.

If there had not been a convenient spike or flake of rock on the ledge, the leader might have used a *thread belay*. This is found where two rocks touch, enabling a rope to be threaded behind them. It is usually most convenient to use a sling but a loop of the climbing rope may be threaded and brought back to the harness. Similarly, a rock which is jammed *tight* in a crack, called a chockstone, may be used to make a *chockstone belay*. The sling or rope is threaded behind the chockstone, as in a thread belay. Trees, which seem to be able to survive on the sheerest mountain face, may also be used as anchors. Dead trees are suspect, so it is wise to check that green leaves are growing to confirm that the tree is alive; this, of course, is not possible in winter.

It may happen that there is no natural rock feature on our ledge to which to anchor the rope. The leader will therefore look for a crack in the rock in which he may be able to insert one of his selection of chocks. If he finds a really firm and snug fit for one or, preferably, two chocks, he can then belay onto that. Chock belays are quick and safe to make and are sometimes preferred to rock anchors. As a last resort, if there is no open crack to take a chock, he might see a narrow crack into which he can hammer a piton. A belay is then made from a carabiner clipped into the eye of the piton.

Whatever type of belay is used an important rule is that a locking carabiner must always be used to secure the climber to the belay. First, a locking carabiner is stronger than an ordinary spring-loaded carabiner, thereby maintaining the strength of the links in our chain. Next, it cannot come open in the considerable agitation and tangle of rope in the event of shock loading during a fall.

Our leader has now belayed himself at the top of the 30 ft slab. He

14 *Leader belayed to a chockstone*

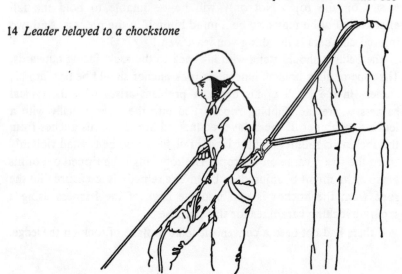

then puts on his belaying gloves, pulls in the rope and calls to No 2 to climb when it becomes tight. No 2 takes off his belaying gloves and starts to climb. The leader does not pull on the rope to help No 2 up the slab. He merely keeps the slack out of the rope, taking it in as No 2 climbs, playing the rope rather as a fisherman plays a fish. The man handling the rope, whether it happens to be the leader or No 2 must always be ready to arrest a fall. This means in particular that his hand must never lose its grip on the inactive rope. There is, therefore, a special way of taking the rope in to achieve this. As the climber moves up a step the rope is taken in and the hand on the inactive rope moves forward. Both ropes are then temporarily gripped by the hand on the active rope while the inactive hand is quickly slid back, ready to take in again. The grip must never be relinquished on the inactive rope whatever the excuse. I was once acting as No 2 when the leader was on a very hard pitch. At that exact moment a live worm chose to fall off the cliff down my open shirt front where it wriggled most disconcertingly. All I could do was a sort of frenzied little war dance on my ledge to express my feelings (and probably those of the worm) but I kept hold of the rope!

There is one very useful lesson No 2 can learn as a beginner. He has been told that the rope is a strong one and that the leader can hold him but there may be a nagging doubt in the back of his mind. When he has moved up a few feet it is an excellent idea if the leader then tells him to stop climbing and to dangle on the rope by taking his hands and feet off the rock. He will see that the rope holds him safely and the leader may add to his confidence by taking his hand off the active rope, holding him with the one hand on the inactive rope. Holding one hand in the air, the leader will say: 'Look, I'm holding you with one hand,' which is very reassuring. To complete this little lesson, it is useful if the leader later climbs down the slab and lets the No 2 hold him, thus finding out for himself what the weight of a man feels like on the rope. At this juncture the leader might usefully demonstrate the use of the Sticht plate, showing how this friction device, attached either directly to the rock anchor or to the second man, further reduces the effort of holding the weight of a man on the rope.

The rope work and the climbing have, so far, been rather over-simplified, just to get us started. If the leader had fallen he would have slithered down the slab to the grass platform with little more than a graze to show for it. The No 2 was just standing on the grass platform, un-belayed. From now on things are going to become more serious and more elaborate precautions must be taken.

The rock steepens above the first pitch into a 60 ft wall, broken here and there with cracks and other lines of weakness in the rock which should provide reasonable foot- and hand-holds. It is obviously a more serious proposition than the easy slab.

On arrival on the ledge the first thing No 2 does is to belay himself to the rock, probably using the same anchor as the leader. He must be well placed to hold the leader should he fall and exert a downward pull on the rope but he must also be able to withstand an upward pull on the rope, for a reason I shall shortly explain. It is therefore necessary for No 2 to belay himself so that he cannot be dragged down off the ledge and desirable that he cannot be jerked into the air in the event of a powerful upward pull. Two anchor points, in opposition, therefore make the ideal belay.

Having changed the belay round (and this can be a tricky operation on a very narrow ledge), the leader is now ready to climb the second pitch. No 2 stands with his back to the rock, paying out the rope.

Because the climb is getting harder the leader decides to minimize the risk of a fall. For example, if he took no intermediate precautions and slipped when he was 25 ft above his No 2, he would, of course, fall the 25 ft down to the No 2, then he would have gone another 25 ft before No 2 arrested him on the rope, a total fall of 50 ft. I once broke my shoulder blade after a fall of 50 ft which I thought was quite enough!

Luckily there is a simple method by which the leader can reduce the effects of a fall. From time to time he puts on a *running belay* or 'gets a runner on' in the jargon. The simplest running belay is made by dropping a sling, with a carabiner already clipped into it, behind a spike or flake in the rock. The climbing rope is then clipped into the carabiner so that it is free to run through it, like a pulley. If the runner is put on, say at shoulder height to the leader, he instantly becomes safe. If he then slips, he will be held without falling, dangling harmlessly against the rock. The use of runners, particularly in conjunction with the modern range of manufactured chocks, has taken a tremendous amount of the risk out of rock climbing, especially when contrasted with the risks the pioneers took before the invention of the carabiner, chock, piton and nylon rope.

The leader must inform his No 2 when he gets a runner on because the shock loading on the rope will then be in an upward instead of a downward direction in the event of a fall, and the No 2 must adjust his stance accordingly. This, or course, is the reason why a double anchor is desirable. No 2 could be jerked into the air and his sling lifted off its rock spike if that was the only belay he had made.

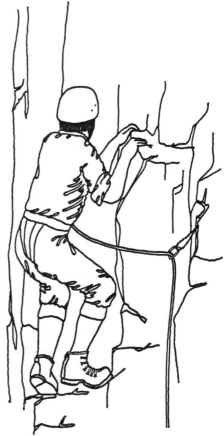

15 *The climbing rope led through a running belay*

The leader must decide how frequently to use running belays, depending on the difficulty of the rock above him and the prevailing conditions. He would use more on wet slippery rock than on dry. It also depends on how he is feeling that particular day. If he is brimming with confidence, he will only use a few runners; if, for some reason, he is feeling off form, he will use quite a lot. It is, however, open to ridicule to use an excessive number of runners on easy rock. It may also be argued that it is irresponsible to ignore a good place for a runner and expose yourself to a fatal fall because you choose to put the arbitrary rules of a sport above the sanctity of human life. These are ethical arguments which endlessly occupy the thoughts, and arguments, of mountaineers. I favour placing a runner every 15–20 ft when the climb is going well. If the climb appears to be unusually easy, runners may be dispensed with altogether; if it appears dauntingly hard runners may be placed every few feet. It is up to you; it is your life.

Pitons are also used for running belays but their use varies with the customs of the country. They are permanently placed at crucial points on rock climbs in the Alps, for instance, but much frowned upon if used on easy climbs in America.

Care must be taken that the rope runs cleanly through the runners or friction will be generated which will result in the leader feeling drag on the rope. He has enough to cope with without this. Drag is most likely if a runner is put tight under an overhang so that the rope is not only bent through a right angle but creates friction where it rubs against the rock face. The solution is to use a long sling for the runner so that the rope hangs clear of the rock. Again, if the route of the climb is a zig-zag, with a runner at each zig and zag, the rope is always being angled and will generate a lot of drag.

Let us assume that our leader is feeling in good form as he leads this 60 ft pitch. He places a runner about every 15 ft, a total of three, before he arrives at his belay on a small rock platform. Having found a good anchor, he belays himself to it, puts on his belaying gloves and takes in the rope to No 2. When the rope cames tight, No 2 unties his own belay and starts to climb. Each time he reaches a runner left by the leader, he removes it and hangs it around his neck or clips it into his harness. When he reaches the leader, he carefully belays, completing this and placing the rope from the leader in the correct belaying position round his waist before the leader unties his own belay. At all times one of the pair must be securely tied to the rock and holding the rope which leads to the other.

Our two climbers are now at the top of the second pitch. The third pitch is something of an unknown quantity. It starts with a small overhang, which looks to be well provided with good holds, but the remainder of the pitch is out of sight. Just at this moment the wind begins to blow quite hard. The leader therefore knows that there are going to be problems of communication. It is an incovenient fact that, particularly in a wind, the voice does not carry at all well up or down a cliff face. Once the leader is above the overhang, the two climbers will not be able to see each other or hear one another very well. This is therefore a good moment to introduce a special set of calls used by climbers. They are brief and have been standardized so that they can usually be understood even if indistinctly heard. They enable the climbers to pass information or instructions quickly and accurately even if they are relative strangers.

Climbing calls

Call	Given by	Meaning
'Belay on'	Leader	The leader has reached his belay and is ready for No 2 rope to No 2.
'That's me'	No 2	Confirms that the rope has tightened to No 2 rather than having jammed in a crack.
'You may climb'	Leader	The leader is in the correct belaying position and ready to hold No 2 if necessary.
'Climbing'	No 2	No 2 has untied his belay and is about to start climbing.
'OK'	Leader	The leader gives the final confirmatory word.
'Slack'	No 2	The leader pays out a little slack into the rope, usually to permit No 2 to climb down a step or two to good holds before having another go.
'Up rope'	No 2	The leader takes in the slack from the rope that has accumulated. Note: avoid using the call 'Take in slack'. It combines two conflicting orders and, if only partially heard, could lead to trouble.
'Tight'	No 2	No 2 is in difficulty. The leader therefore tightens the rope in anticipation of No 2 coming off the rock.
'Tension'	Leader or No 2	The leader or No 2 is in serious trouble and may come off the rock at any moment. The man on the belay braces himself to arrest the fall. This is not usually very serious if No 2 comes off but can be the start

		of a bad accident if the leader falls.
'Runner on'	Leader	The leader has made a running belay. No 2 will now anticipate an upward rather than a downward pull in the event of a fall and adjusts his stance accordingly.
'Thirty (twenty, etc) feet'	No 2	No 2 is warning the leader that he only has 30 (20, etc) feet of climbing rope left so he must find a belay within that distance.
'I'm there'	Leader	The leader has reached his belay and No 2 may relax a little but he may not yet untie his belay.
'Off belay'	Leader	The leader is now secure in his belay spot; No 2 may untie his belay.
'Rock'	Any climber or hill walker	Watch out; a dislodged stone is bouncing down the mountainside.

Across and Down

Let us assume that our two climbers, communicating effectively by means of the climbing calls, successfully climb the third pitch. The fourth pitch is a short one but it is what is known as a *traverse*. This means that the route, instead of continuing upwards, goes more or less horizontally.

The most obvious problem on a traverse is the lack of protection to a possibly inexperienced No 2. Hitherto the leader's rope has been directly above No 2 so that, in the event of a slip, he would merely dangle on the end of the rope until he was able to sort himself out and have another go, possibly with a bit of a pull on the rope to help him. If No 2 falls on a traverse he will naturally 'do a pendulum' which could well send him crashing into the rock and cause an injury.

The considerate leader will therefore only undertake a traverse if he is quite confident that the pitch is well within the ability of his No 2. He will futher minimize the risk by placing runners much more frequently than he would normally. This, of course, much reduces the radius of any pendulum on the part of No 2. On our particular climb, the leader knows that the traverse is a very easy one and our inexperienced No 2 makes it without difficulty.

The next pitch, the fifth, is the last and here we will permit a little drama to enter our story. This final pitch is a very smooth slab almost entirely devoid of good holds. The leader knows that he will have to depend entirely on the friction between the tiny holds on the dry rock and the rubber soles of his boots. He is therefore keeping a very wary eye on a dark rain cloud moving up the valley, hoping that his luck will hold. It does not. Just as he arrives at the top pitch the rain starts and the slab is soon streaming with water. He makes the correct decision that the pitch is now unclimbable and that he must retreat down the cliff face. The two climbers could climb down, No 2 going first, always protected from above by the leader's rope. This is a perfectly normal procedure which mountaineers regularly undertake. However, the leader decides to use the alternative method of descent, *roping down*, also called *abseiling* (German derivation) or rappelling (French and American usage).

In this method the climbers use a doubled rope to lower themselves, pulling it down after them. They repeat the process until the rock face is descended. If carried out quickly and efficiently, a safe and rapid descent can be made down a sheer and unclimbable face. The skillful selection and preparation of anchor points is the key to safety and success. In order that the doubled rope may be pulled down easily it is fed through a sling which is attached to the rock and abandoned. It is of paramount importance that this sling is safely fixed—which is easier said than done—because an accident while abseiling is almost certain to be a very serious one. Rappelling is something that should be thoroughly rehearsed under training conditions because when it is carried out in practice the mountaineers are often in retreat, maybe tired at the end of a long day, and in worsening weather; in other words when they are most accident prone. On the other hand some abseils are foreseen because they are the recognized method of descent on a particular route and are forewarned in the guidebooks.

When rappelling is preplanned, as it usually is in the higher mountains, a special, extra long and thin rope of between 200 and 300 feet is carried specifically for abseiling. The climbing rope is retained as a safety rope with one of the climbers always belayed. In an emergency the climbing rope may be used for rappelling although this is intrinsically dangerous because it cannot then be used as the safety rope.

Any anchor which is suitable for a belay—a rock spike, flake, thread, chockstone, manufactured chock or piton—is also suitable for an abseil anchor. In rappelling there is the advantage that the pull can only

16 *Roping down or rappelling using the*
classic method

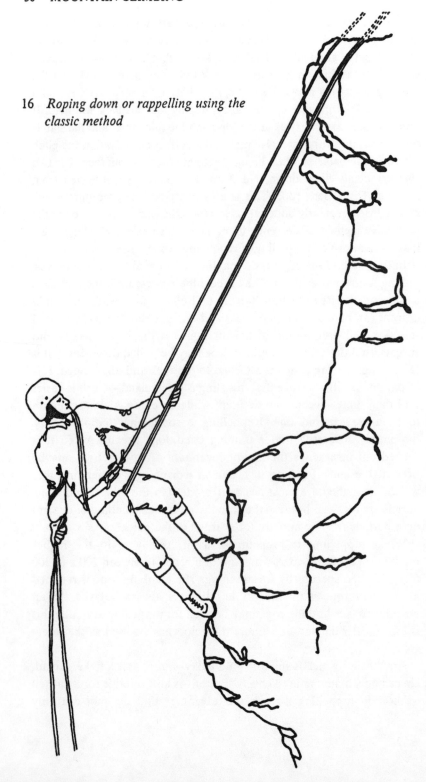

come downwards and the strain should never approach that of a falling leader. It will merely be the weight of a climber lowering himself, possibly in a jerky manner. It is usual to carry a spare length of nylon webbing or thin nylon rope specifically for making rappel slings. An appropriate length can then be cut off to make a sling (a double sling is better) to fit the selected anchor point. If the rock at the anchor point has sharp edges, it should be padded, with a handkerchief if necessary, to avoid any danger of the rope being severed while under strain. In an unplanned rappel, ordinary slings may, of course, be used.

If there is too much friction on the rope it is very difficult to pull down. A sufficiently long sling should therefore be used so that the rope does not snag but has a clean pull down the rock face.

The anchor point having been selected, the sling must be fixed to the mountain and the doubled rope fed through it. The quickest method is to find the centre of the rope, which should anyway be marked, and tie the sling round the rope there. Alternatively, the centre may be found and the rope passed through the sling to its middle point. The rope must then be thrown down and this is where it is only too easy to get into an unholy mess. Even though it might appear to be neatly coiled, the thing not to do is throw the whole rope down the cliff in one bunch. It is certain to get in a tangle. Each half of the doubled rope should be thrown separately having first been very neatly sorted out and coiled.

The doubled rope is now in position ready for descent which may be made by three methods; the classic, the standard or the descender. Gloves should be worn.

In the *classic* method, stand facing in to the rock. Take the doubled rope coming from the abseil sling, lead it between the legs, round the right thigh, up across the chest over the left shoulder and down under the right armpit, to end with a turn round the forearm. The climber is now safely enwrapped in the rope and can slowly lower himself even over an overhanging rock and he will be held in a sitting position without any tendency to turn upside down and fall out of the ropes but should not be undertaken by beginners without expert instruction. It is all delightfully simple and no extra equipment is needed. There is, however, a major snag—rope friction. The rope bites into the shoulder and the rump. This is not only painful but can cause a nasty rope burn.

Much of the friction may be removed from the body by using the *standard* method which only requires a locking carabiner and a sling,

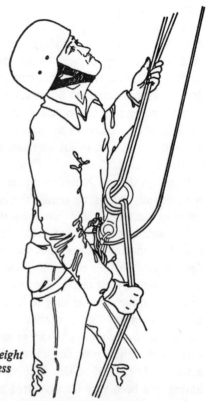

17 *Roping down using a figure-of-eight descender attached to a sit-harness*

preferably a long webbing sling. The sling is made either into a figure-of-eight loop and a leg inserted into each loop or a more elaborate 'nappy' sling with each leg in a loop and a third loop going round the waist. Facing the anchor, the doubled rope is clipped into the carabiner, the lock tightened and turned away from the rope. The rope is then led over the left shoulder, across the back to the right forearm where a turn is taken. Much of the rope friction will now be absorbed in the carabiner. Care must be taken that the parka is well tucked in around the waist because it is possible for a fold in the cloth to catch in the rope and get jammed in the carabiner.

The *descender* method is the most comfortable of all, particularly if used with a thigh harness. The descender is in the form of a metal figure-of-eight. A loop of the doubled rope is pushed through the larger ring from the top and led behind the shank. The smaller ring of the descender is then clipped into the harness or a sling (as described for the standard method) with a locking carabiner. The doubled rope is then controlled with the lower, right, hand and the whole procedure should be comfortable and enjoyable. Again, watch out for loose clothing getting jammed in the descender.

A word of warning: the descender is designed to be used with a double rope. If a single rope is used it may not generate enough friction and this can be dangerous. An extra source of friction must therefore be added, for example by running the rope from the descender over the shoulder and round the arm, as in the classic method.

When rappelling the descent should be slow and controlled. To minimize strain on the anchor point, jumps or violent stops should be avoided. Never go abseiling over an overhang unless you can see that the rope safely reaches a ledge or you may be left dangling in space unable to get back up!

Before leaving ropework, two variations in climbing teamwork should be mentioned. If two climbers are on a climb which both are capable of leading, they will usually *lead through* which is quicker and shares the pleasure of leading. When one climber leads a pitch he, of course, belays and brings up his friend. Instead of changing over the belay, the second climber carries straight on through and leads the second pitch. This procedure is continued all the way up.

Mountaineers can also climb three on a rope but progress is slower because only one can climb at a time. The usual procedure is for the leader to climb the first pitch and then bring up No 2. The leader then climbs the second pitch, belays, and tells No 2 to bring up No 3. When No 3 is up the first pitch and belayed, the leader brings up No 2 and then climbs the third pitch, and so on. Four, or even more, can climb together but this becomes progressively more cumbersome and is not really to be recommended.

Chapter 5

Rock Climbing Technique

In rock climbing, as in every human activity, each individual develops his own style. 'Style is the man himself,' as the French say. A person's rock climbing style is a reflection of his personality and probably depends more on his mental than on his physical make-up. It is an obvious disadvantage to be fat and unfit but mere shape seems to make little difference. Tall or short men, light or heavy, all can make excellent climbers and adapt their style to suit their build. You simply cannot tell by outside appearances whether a person has the aptitude.

Only a few of the hardest climbs call for superhuman strength, usually in the fingers. Success in climbing is therefore predominantly a mental problem. A person who brims over with determination and confidence in the face of difficulty almost certainly has the making of a natural climber. A person who lacks these qualities is unlikely to become a successful leader although he might enjoy the sport in the less demanding role of second man.

Although style comes through practice rather than by reading a book about it, there are certain guidelines to good technique which should be studied. It is also useful to learn the jargon used by climbers to describe rock formations and climbing techniques.

There is an immense difference between the leader and No 2. They are almost playing different games. The leader bears the ultimate weight of responsibility and it is therefore of paramount importance that his judgement should be sound. If he makes a serious miscalculation he is going to pay for it, possibly by suffering a serious fall. In almost every move he makes his judgement is involved. By contrast, No 2's main contribution is to be punctilious about his safety measures and, by a robust yet realistic attitude, to encourage the leader to do his best but to discourage him if necessary from pushing his luck too far. When it comes to the actual climbing, he has no choice other than to follow the leader's footsteps, always with the reassuring safety of the top rope. If No 2 slips and falls, it seldom matters. Climbers are not rigidly divided into leaders and No 2s. The most enjoyable climbing is done by pairs of climbers of more or less equal ability who climb together regularly and work very much as a team. They will usually discuss problems and share both the judgement and the leading.

Judgement is a continuous process and begins long before the actual climbing starts. A pair of climbers may have been reading about a certain route in a guidebook (more about guidebooks shortly) and debating whether they should try it. On the morning of the start they will be very aware of the weather. If it is raining or snowing, they will vary their program accordingly. They must also relate the length and difficulty of the climb to the daylight hours available and to their own ability. If the route is well within their ability they will probably polish it off quite quickly. If it is at the very limit of their ability, they may take a long time over it. If, in addition, the route is very long, they will have to consider whether they have enough daylight time. If not, they may have to plan a bivouac. This involves carrying food, a lightweight cooking stove and a sleeping bag. They must also assess the amount of rope and other equipment required for a particular route. There might, for example, be a number of rappels necessary, perhaps on the descent. Is it necessary to carry a separate rappel rope?

The foregoing are basically objective considerations. The subjective ones cannot be listed but they are equally important. If our climbers attended their climbing club annual get-together and were drinking beer almost until dawn, their climbing standards have probably come down a grade or two! A climber might just be feeling 'down' for no very identifiable reason. We all have our off days. It is important to recognize them and not to push yourself if you feel that your reservoir of resolve is at a low ebb. The reverse also applies. You might wake up on a sunny morning feeling like a young Alexander the Great, ready to conquer the known world. That is the day to have a go at a route a grade harder than anything you have previously led. It is really all in the mind.

The need for good judgement is at its greatest when the leader is attempting a rock route which has never been climbed before, or if he is on a mountaineering expedition to a virgin peak. Few climbers, particularly in their early stages, are in this situation and most of the problems of judgement can be solved for them by reading the rock climbing guidebook to the area. Guidebooks exist for almost every area where climbing has been carried out for any length of time.

The guidebooks are mines of information and are available in most shops selling climbing equipment. In the front there is usually general advice about where to stay and where the best climbing is to be found. Any special local conditions will be mentioned. The bulk of the book is taken up with detailed descriptions of each route. A diagram or annotated photograph will indicate where the route is to be found on the crag. The difficulty usually will be graded. This is a vital piece of information because the leader will immediately know whether the route is within his ability or not. There will be some general remarks about the route: whether it follows a fine or a rather messy line up the cliff; whether the rock tends to be firm or liable to break; if there are any snags such as a danger from stonefall or a proneness for the rocks to be wet or greasy; and so on. A detailed description will be given of the start of the climb so that the climbers can positively identify (not always easy) that they are in fact at the foot of the climb in question.

The route description may take the form of a continuous narrative with detailed information about only the more difficult pitches. Alternatively, the routes may be described pitch by pitch. Here is a typical description of a second pitch:

(2) 45 feet. From the right edge of the platform, climb the slab delicately for 15 feet on small holds to the foot of a crack. This is awkward to start on rounded, greasy holds but after 10 feet good holds lead easily to a ledge. Flake belay.

It can be seen that the guidebook not only tells the leader how long the pitch is, but a clear hint is given where to expect the difficulties, and their nature. 'Delicate' means that the holds are very small and the climber will have to depend on good balance. 'Awkward' means that the holds are not at all where he would like them to be and an out-of-balance, strenuous heave will probably be needed to surmount the foot of the crack which, to add to the difficulties, tends to be greasy at that spot. Once arrived on the ledge the leader will look for the flake belay.

The degree of the difficulty described in the above pitch must be related to the overall standard of the climb. In America there are four grading systems: adjectival, N.C.C.S., decimal and U.I.A.A. This would seem confusing, but fortunately the methods can be correlated by use of the following table:

Correlation of Common Systems for Rating Individual Pitch Difficulty

Adjective	N.C.C.S.	Decimal	U.I.A.A.	Description
Easy	F1 F2	1 2 & 3	I II	A scramble, where use of the hands is necessary and a beginner might need a rope.
Moderate	F3	4 5	III— III	Definitely roped climbing but the holds are big and the angle easy.
Moderately difficult	F4	5.1	III+	Technical climbing starts here. The route may be steep, the holds small, and proper rock climbing technique is needed to climb in safety. Those who are not natural climbers find this their top limit of difficulty.
Difficult	F5	5.3 5.4 5.5	IV IV+ V—	Harder or more strenuous than previous, but the difficulties do not usually go on for too long. Experienced climbers move slowly and deliberately here.
Very difficult	F6 F7 F8	5.6 5.7 5.8	V V+ VI—	Hard or strenuous climbs on which the difficulties are often sustained. Special footwear, such as PAs, will often be preferred.
Extremely difficult	F9 F10 F11	5.9 5.10 5.11	VI VI+	Demanding climbs of sustained difficulty. The very hardest climbs which require either superb technique or great strength—sometimes both.

Of the four systems, the U.I.A.A. is internationally accepted and is the oldest in origin. The decimal system was devised in the 1940s and early 1950s by California climbers for use on Yosemite rock. The N.C.C.S. method is of more recent origin. Neither the decimal nor the N.C.C.S. systems enjoy any following outside North America.

Whatever the system (or systems) employed by a guidebook or by local climbers, a person quickly adjusts to it and relates it to his own ability. They are, of course, a major contribution to safety because they enable a mountaineer to climb within his ability and to graduate slowly and systematically to harder routes as his prowess improves.

Good Climbing Style

Having arrived at the start of a rock climb a party of climbers will rope up and, if the ground below the start is steep, No 2 will belay himself to the rock. The leader then attends to his most important duty—which is not to start climbing but to *use his eyes and head*. He must study the pitch in detail, noting where the good holds and possible resting places are, checking if there are any wet or greasy patches or any suspect rock. He will look for spikes, flakes or cracks where he might expect to fix running belays. Only when his mental assessment of the pitch is completed will he start to climb.

No two climbers will climb a pitch in exactly the same way, using precisely the same style. There are however a number of principles which are an aid to good style. It is very important to maintain good balance. The instinctive thing for a beginner to do is to lean in to the rock and to depend almost entirely on heaving himself up by arm strength. This is bad style for several reasons: first, on many climbs there are insufficient handholds, making the climber depend on footholds; and the legs are far stronger than the arms in any case and should be made to do most of the work, thus conserving arm strength for the few occasions when it is really needed.

There are other reasons as well. If the climber keeps his body in a relaxed, upright position, with his weight over his feet, he is in balance and there is little strain on his arms. Also, he has an unobstructed view of his feet. If he leans into the rock and reaches high for his hand-holds, he is flattened against the rock face and cannot see the foot-holds, which are vital.

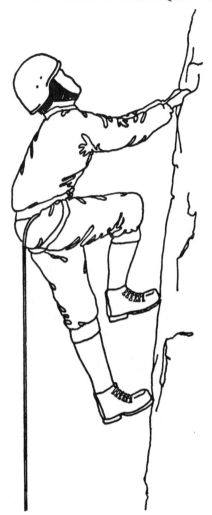

18 *Good balance position*

If you watch an experienced climber on a pitch where there are plenty of holds, not necessarily big ones, you will notice that he climbs with his hands kept relatively low. He will only reach high above his head, to the limit of his reach, if there is no alternative. He will take small steps, which will give the impression of effortless climbing, rather than taking big steps, reaching high with his hands, and going up in a series of convulsive heaves. This latter is over-tiring and must be avoided, particularly on very long routes on big mountains.

Good footwork is vital and is often the key to the harder climbs. The foot must be moved from one hold to the next carefully and deliberately and placed very accurately on the hold, not just jabbed onto the rock. The heels should be kept down, which reduces any tendency of the boot to slip. If the climber reaches very high, his heels come up and he increases the chance of his foot slipping.

Holds should be tested, even on routes which are regularly climbed. This is done by pulling firmly on the hand-holds and by giving foot-holds a light kick with the toe to check that they do not move. As a further precaution against a hold breaking or a foot slipping the rule of 'three point climbing' should be followed. This means that only one limb should be moved at a time, leaving the other three on safe holds. In other words, only move one hand or one foot at a time. Never move an arm and a leg together. If there are three points on the rock and one breaks, at least two remain. But if a climber, say, moves an arm and leg together and at that moment his foot slips, or his hand-hold breaks, then he will probably fall.

The difficulties on a rock pitch are usually obvious and are probably mentioned in the route description. The best thing to do is to climb to a good resting place below the hard part, choosing a spot with good footholds where you can stand in easy balance. From there the rock should be studied and a plan of campaign, a probable series of moves, worked out mentally in advance. Having had a careful look and think, and not before, the difficulties should be tackled with all the determination that can be mustered. The wrong thing to do is to go on climbing until you are almost stuck before you pause to sum up the situation.

The Mountain Landscape

There are certain specific techniques which have been evolved to surmount the various characteristic configurations of the rock. Climbers use their own jargon to describe both the rock formations and the techniques; these we should now consider.

Rock formations are much influenced by the nature of the bedrock, in other words by the geology of the area. Rocks are divided into three main groups: igneous, metamorphic and sedimentary. Although most of the land surface of the world is underlaid with sedimentary rock, igneous and metamorphic rocks are much in evidence in mountain ranges. What climbers most want from climbing rock is that, above all, it should be firm. Brittle or loose rock is both unpleasant and dangerous to climb on.

It is an advantage if the texture of the rock is rough, like sandpaper. This gives plenty of friction which is particularly useful in enabling the boots to get a good grip on sloping foot-holds. Rough rock also continues to give good friction when wet.

Granite, an igneous rock, is probably most closely associated with mountaineering. It occurs in many of the mountain areas of the world and is usually superbly rough and reliable to climb on. It can, however, become shattered, particularly as a result of frost and it can be encountered in a decomposed and unreliable state. Gabbro is another wonderfully rough igneous rock. Other good igneous climbing rocks include rhyolite and dolerite.

Of the metamorphic rocks, gneiss (somewhat similar in appearance to granite) is probably the best to climb on. Slates and schists are also metamorphic.

Sedimentary rocks, with their characteristic layering, can vary widely. Gritstone is firm, rough and rounded; limestone tends to be hard, smooth and slippery when wet. Much of the loose, rotten rock in mountain formations is sedimentary.

A *buttress* is a large and distinctive rock feature which stands out from a mountainside. A *ridge* or *arête* is a sharp edge which runs down a mountainside and is a major feature. A less well defined edge on a buttress is called a *rib*. A fairly smooth and flat rock face is called a *slab* if it is less than about 75°, a *wall* if it is between 75° and the vertical. An *overhang* is rock that steepens beyond the vertical. Fissures are subdivided into three categories: if they are too narrow to squeeze into they are called *cracks*. If the climber can get into the fissure and use holds on both sides they are called *chimneys*. Wider than that they become *gullies*. A *corner* is where the rock walls rise more or less at right angles to each other; where a corner is more open, resembling an open book, it becomes a dyhedral. An ample, flat break on a rock face is called a *platform;* if it is more narrow it becomes a *ledge*. A narrow ledge with a smooth wall rising behind it is a *mantleshelf.*

Specialized techniques

Most rock climbing takes place on open faces where it is possible to climb quite naturally, usually on an obvious combination of holds.

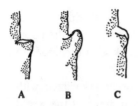

19   *Types of hand-hold: A Flat. B Incut or 'Thank Godder'. C Rounded*

However, rocks come in an infinite variety of shapes and sizes, some of which require specialized techniques to surmount them.

Holds can be flat, incut or rounded. Incut hand-holds are wonderfully reassuring. The fingers sink deeply into the recess and the climber feels safe. Really good incut holds are nicknamed *thank Godders,* occasionally *jughandles,* abbreviated to 'jugs.' You can often hear the heartfelt relief in a leader's voice when he has climbed a hard bit and then shouts down to his No 2: 'I've got the 'thank Godder!'

Not all hand-holds are in the horizontal plane where they assist the climber to pull up. Vertical holds can be very useful. Sometimes a sideways push on a *pressure hold* keeps the climber nicely in balance while he makes the next move. A small vertical hold can be used for a

20 *Types of hold: A Pressure hold. B Side pull. C Undercut hold. D Pinch grip*

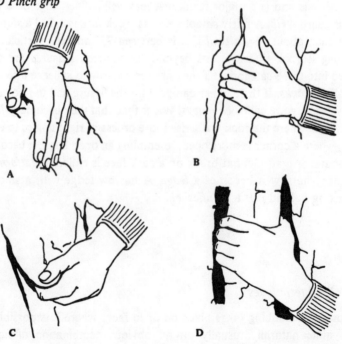

A   B

21 *Hand jams: A Open hand. B Fist*

side pull usually for the same purpose. The bottom edge of a flake can provide *undercut holds*. The climber can then pull down against the counterpressure of a foot-hold, holding himself safely onto the rock while the other leg or hand is moved up to the next hold. Sometimes a small bulge in the rock can be squeezed between the thumb and fingers in a *pinch grip*. If a hand-hold is so small that only one finger can get a good grip on it, it is best to use the middle finger which most people find is the strongest.

Cracks and chimneys are frequently climbed. Even if a narrow, vertical crack is smooth and devoid of holds it may be climbed by jamming hands or feet or possibly both. If it is very narrow the open hand can be inserted and jammed with the knuckles against one side and the fingertips and heel of the hand exerting the counterpressure against the other. In wider cracks a fist can be made which will jam and support the whole weight. The toe of the boot can be jammed in the crack or, if it is wider, the boot inserted sideways and twisted slightly to jam.

A narrow chimney, in other words a crack into which the body will just fit sideways, can be exhausting to climb but even here technique will help. It is climbed by a wriggling movement with hips and shoulders. The principle is to gain a few inches by wriggling and then to work out a means of jamming so that the height gained is held until the next successful, and tiring, wriggle. It may be possible to jam the boot across the crack or, if the crack is too wide, to use the two boots in combination. It may also be possible to jam with the forearms.

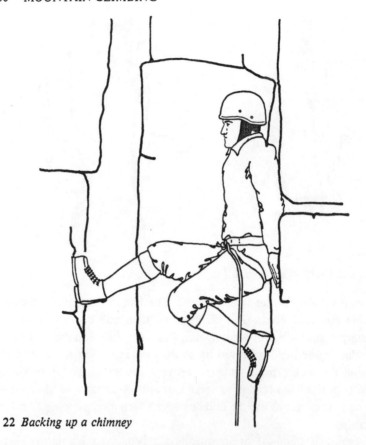

22 *Backing up a chimney*

A wider crack is usually easier, enabling the climber to place both his feet on one side and jam by pressing his seat against the rock in a comfortable, resting position. Progress is made by moving one foot and pressing it against the rock under the seat, at the same time pressing upwards with the heel of the hands. The climber will lift himself anything up to a foot whereupon the process is repeated. This is called *backing up*. This method will not work if the chimney is wider than the length of the climber's leg. In this case it is necessary to *bridge* or *straddle* across the chimney, feet and arms stretched wide apart, an arm and foot on each side. The chimney can be climbed merely by exerting strong pressure on both arms and feet. However, both hand jamming in cracks and using arm and foot pressure in chimneys can be tiring and one of the principles of good climbing is to preserve strength. If there are natural holds they should always be used in preference to pressure holds. Finally, before burying an arm in a crack or your whole body in a chimney (both of

23 *Straddling up a wide chimney*

which make you feel safe) take a good look at the outside wall. Although the climbing is more exposed, a route up the outside will be less tiring and more elegant.

Most cracks that can be climbed by hand jamming can also be climbed using a *layback* but this is usually very strenuous. In a layback the arms and legs are worked in opposition and because the arms are much weaker than the legs, they tire first. The hands grasp one edge of the crack, the feet being placed against the other edge to exert their counterpressure. Hands and feet are then moved in sequence, one limb at a time. It often takes boldness to commit yourself to a layback, especially if there is a big drop beneath. The best thing to do, once committed, is to go as fast as you reasonably can while your strength lasts. The principle of speed should also be applied to climbing overhangs and making *hand traverses*. On an overhang, the weight inevitably comes on the arms. It is no place to hang around! A hand traverse, not often met, is a thin crack or a flake leading sideways which offers small incut hand-holds but which is practically devoid of foot-holds. The climber moves across, virtually

24 *Climbing a vertical crack by the layback method*

suspended from his fingers, but using whatever meagre foot-holds which may exist to take a little of the weight on the legs.

Many narrow ledges present mantleshelf problems. In other words they are backed by a smooth wall so that the climber has to gain the ledge without the assistance of thank Godders on the ledge or on the wall behind. Assuming the ledge has a sharp edge, the climber gets both hands onto it. He then works his feet up as far as he can. Now comes the big effort: he pulls hard on his arms to raise his torso and at the same time changes his hands from a pull up to a push up, straightening his arms. Then one foot is lifted to the ledge and the climber gingerly stands up, just keeping in balance. There is a strong temptation to use the knees but this should be resisted because the climber would then end up kneeling on the ledge still faced with the problem of trying to get onto his feet. Also he might be asked, sarcastically: 'Why are you saying your prayers?' A supple man can normally place his foot on a hold where he can place his knee and should always do so.

If a climber, perhaps faced with a short smooth wall, is quite unable to climb it, he may call for *combined tactics*. He will belay and bring up his No 2. When No 2 has in turn belayed, he will then climb up on to his shoulders, and possibly stand on the poor fellow's head, to gain some good holds which had been beyond his reach.

Climbing Down

Descent of a rock face using a series of rappels sounds attractively quick, easy and safe. As we have seen, this is not entirely true, particularly if the party is not well practiced in rappelling. A lack of suitably spaced anchor points, a high wind, the absence of a long rappel rope (which easily happens if the rappel was not planned) can all combine to make descent by rappel slow and worrying. On easy rock it is usually faster to climb down.

Climbing down is therefore a vital part of mountaineering training. Climbing big mountains often involves the ascent of a hard route followed by descent of an easier route which nonetheless requires sustained climbing down. The best advice, frequently ignored, is that in his early stages a climber should do just as much climbing down as ascending.

We have already described the ropework in climbing down which is a simple reversal of the ascent with the leader always coming down last so that his No 2 is safeguarded from above by the rope.

Greater responsibility falls on No 2 in a descent, particularly over unfamiliar rock. He must select the belay points and he must also place the running belays to minimize the danger to the leader when it is his turn to climb down.

There is also a difference in climbing technique. When ascending, the climber sees all the foot-holds in front of his nose as he passes them. In climbing down he is looking below his feet for the next foot-holds and on very steep rock this is difficult. The best advice is 'hands low'. This enables the climber to lean out and look down and also to lower himself to his arms reach before he then works his hands down low again. It is disconcerting always looking down, and many climbers feel uneasy descending. There is a good saying, which certainly applies to easy and medium climbs, 'Never make a move you cannot reverse'. On the hardest climbs this saying becomes something of a pious hope!

Chapter 6

Artificial* and Solo Climbing

Rock climbing can be *free* or *artificial*. In free climbing the rope, karabiners, pitons, chocks and slings are used for protection only, upward progress being achieved by use of the arms, legs and any other part of the anatomy the climber can bring into contact with the rock! In artificial climbing pitons, chocks and lightweight ladders are used for support where none is provided by nature. Climbing ethics dictate that artificial aid should never be used if it can be dispensed with. It therefore follows that artificial pitches should only be found on the very hardest, and usually steepest, rock which cannot be climbed free even at the standard of Extremely Difficult.

There is a wide spectrum of artificial climbing. It is also a subject that generates some heated controversy. The purists postulate that there is more than enough rock in the world that can be climbed free. They go on to say that pitons damage and disfigure the rock and reduce the sport to an ignoble version of steeplejacking. Protagonists of artificial climbing counter that their routes trace some of the finest and boldest lines up otherwise unclimbable faces and merely add to the sum total of worthy ascents. The climber must make up his own mind.

Artificial climbing in its most reasonable form occurs in a situation where a fine free route is blocked by a small section of obviously unclimbable rock. This is surmounted by placing a piton or two which are then used as additional hand- or foot-holds to make the whole route possible. Climbers are, inevitably, not content to leave it at that. The skill of artificial climbing has now been developed into a sophisticated technique with its own hardware which enables the exponent to climb massive and bald walls, unthinkable as free climbs. It has reached its ultimate in America on the huge, smooth and very steep granite walls of the famous

* Also known as *direct aid* climbing

54

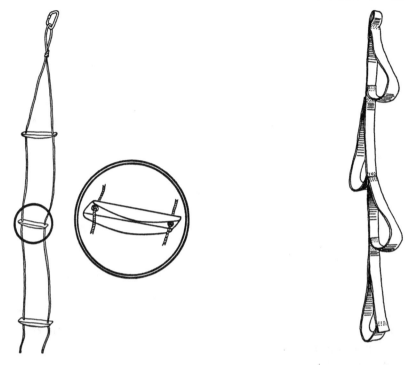

25 *Stirrup*   *Webbing ladder*

Yosemite Valley. Artificial routes of great length and difficulty have been climbed in Yosemite, sometimes requiring the climbers to bivouac in hammocks suspended over space from pitons. However, the hey-day of piton-ing is probably past. Current thinking, particularly in Yosemite, is that artificial routes should now only be climbed if chocks can be used exclusively in the place of the damaging and rust-generating metal piton. Artificial climbs are graded A1 to A5 in ascending order of difficulty.

For artificial climbing a good selection of pitons is needed together with a piton hammer. This hammer has a flat head and, usually, a short pick. Like all climbing hardware, it must be attached to the body with a light sling. Finally about four *stirrups* or lightweight rope ladders with rungs are needed but nylon *webbing ladders,* with foot loops instead of rungs, are marginally preferable. No 2 may also carry *ascenders,* devices which enable him to climb the rope to his leader without too much effort.

Before trying an artificial climb it is essential to know how to place pitons correctly, a skill that only comes through practice. Pitons come in many shapes and sizes and some of them have been given curious names such as *bongs* or *rurps*. However, the three most commonly used are blade, channel-shaped or Z-shaped in cross section. All have a strengthened shoulder to take the shock of hammering and have a hole large enough to clip a karabiner through. The best pitons are made from chrome molybdenum or other high quality spring steel. They do not deform even when hammered into very hard rock, as mild steel pitons do. They may safely be reused many times.

When a piton is hammered into a crack, the hammer blows should make a progressively higher ringing note which indicates that the piton is biting in firmly. If it makes a hollow note it means that it is loose and unsafe. A piton should normally he hammered right home until its shoulder is against the rock. Horizontal cracks provide the strongest anchor against a downward pull on the rope. Obviously pitons placed in vertical cracks will more easily pull down and out under shock loading. However, in artificial climbing the piton is only required to take the weight of the climber, who may bounce up and down a little, possibly putting a strain of double his weight on the piton. For this reason pitons merely used to support the weight of the climber should be relatively lightly hammered in, to make them easier to remove. Periodically on an artificial pitch a piton should be used as a running belay, for protection in the event of a fall, and this should be hammered well home in a horizontal crack. An evening's practice in piton-placing on a boulder with some cracks in it is strongly recommended before an artificial climb is attempted. Practice is also needed in getting them out. This is done by hammering sideways, first one way then the other, until they became loose. It is easy to drop a piton in getting it out. It should therefore be safeguarded with an old karabiner and a light sling.

A completely smooth wall, utterly devoid of holds or cracks, can still be climbed using *expansion bolts*. A rawlplug type drill is used to gouge a hole an inch deep in the rock into which an engineer's bolt is screwed. A

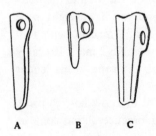

A   B   C

26 *Pitons: A Channel. B Short blade.*
   C Z-shaped or 'Leeper'

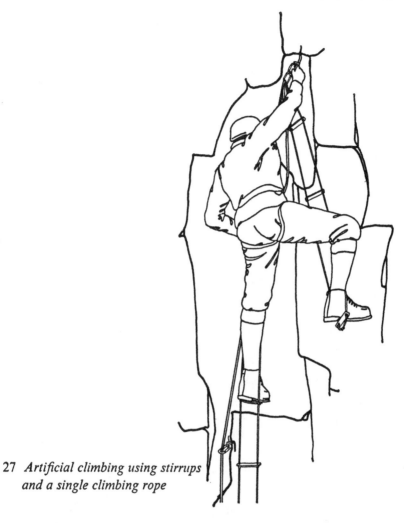

27 *Artificial climbing using stirrups*
    and a single climbing rope

tape ladder can then be suspended from the bolt. This is generally regarded as taking aid climbing too far and 'bolting', as it is called, is very much a minority activity.

The basic procedure for artificial climbing is that the leader, on encountering rock that cannot be climbed free, hammers in a piton as high as he can possibly reach. He hangs a tape ladder or a stirrup from this piton, climbs it, and then hammers in another piton, again as high as he can reach. He hangs another ladder from the second piton and climbs it, repeating this process until the pitch is climbed.

The leader usually attaches a short sling to his harness which he clips into each piton in turn, to support him firmly while he is placing the next piton. For protection he also clips the climbing rope into each piton, in a series of running belays. To reduce clutter at the piton, two carabiners are clipped into the top of each ladder. This enables the climbing rope to run more freely.

The rope management in artificial climbing needs careful handling and it is quite easy to get into a tangle. Lots of practice and teamwork are necessary for really smooth operation. It might sound deceptively easy, just moving up safely from one piton to the next. This is not so. Piton hammering is extremely tiring on the arms. Also, there is a constant need to hold yourself in balance which again tires the arms. One way of conserving strength is to curl a foot backwards into the ladder and squat back on it, in relative comfort and in balance.

The unfortunate No 2 often has a hard and tiring time, especially on overhanging rock. He has to remove the pitons in a situation where he would prefer to be hanging onto them and tends to swing away from the rock if he does not! Often he will not try to repeat the leader's movements but come up the rope on his ascenders, removing the pitons as he reaches them. To add to his troubles, if the climb is on a very steep and smooth wall, he may have to belay his leader while standing on ladders rather than relaxing on a belay on a nice wide ledge.

There is obviously considerable scope for variation in the rope and ladder management in artificial climbing and individuals work out their favorite techniques, some preferring to use a double rope. It is always the aim to use as little artificial aid as possible and there is always the chance that a really brilliant climber will come along and lead the route free, making the artificial climbers look a little foolish.

Solo Climbing

Solo climbing, with a minimum of equipment, or even none at all, is the very antithesis of artificial climbing and is an increasing vogue, perhaps a reaction against the over-security of too many chocks and pitons.

Some solo climbers carry a short length of rope which they can tie into a loop and rig a makeshift running belay. It then gives them the ability to attain partial protection on especially difficult moves. Others carry a couple of carabiners which they can clip into pitons which are already in place.

Solo climbing is also controversial. Some say it involves an unjustifiable risk where even the tiniest slip can prove fatal because it will go unchecked by the rope. It undoubtedly requires courage and confidence and is perhaps the ultimate expression of individualism and therefore to be admired. It should not be undertaken lightly.

Chapter 7

Snow and Ice Climbing

The ambitious mountaineer will not be content to limit himself to rock climbing on his local crags but will seek to widen his horizons by visiting some of the great ranges of North America or the world, the Rockies, Alaska, or even in these days of easy and relatively cheap air travel the peaks of the Alps, New Zealand, the Caucasus, Andes or Himalayas. These ranges, and many others, contain glaciers and snowfields which require special equipment and techniques to climb them. The technique is generally described as alpine climbing and normally takes place in summer.

Snow and ice climbing is, however, also practiced in lower ranges in the winter, the White Mountains being a well known example. In this type of mountain range, even if there are no glaciers or permanent snowfields, there are difficulties enough. The winter days are short (and the winter nights are very long and cold if you are unlucky enough to be benighted!). As well as snow and ice the climber has to cope with snow-spattered rocks where all the holds are covered.

It is also possible to climb the easier snow peaks in the higher ranges in the winter or, preferably, early spring. The Alps, unlike American mountains, are particularly suitable for this because the network of alpine huts provides shelter, thus avoiding the necessity to camp. Skis are used to reach the foot of the steep snow and the sport is described as ski-mountaineering.

Some of the hardest alpine routes have been climbed in winter but this is a desperately hard undertaking, the ultimate in the craft of mountaineering. A notable recent achievement was the first winter ascent of the famous north face of the Eiger. This climb was, or course, much harder under winter conditions, but it was safer to the extent that falling stones which are such a hazard in summer were no problem because all the rocks were cemented fast in the grip of frost.

The interplay of snowfield, glacier and rock buttress creates a grandeur which delights the mountaineer. Snow and ice climbing is part of the very essence of the sport of mountaineering and many eastern climbers think the long journey to the West, or the nearest glaciated range, is fully justified by the pleasure derived from climbing the great snowfields. It does, however, demand steadiness and the power to concentrate over long periods in a situation where there is far less security than is enjoyed when rock climbing. It does not always follow that a brilliant rock climber is a good snow and ice man, or vice-versa. To some extent they call for different qualities: a quick burst of all-out effort to surmount a few really hard moves on rock, but long, nerve-shredding passages of step cutting up steep snow or ice.

Equipment

The **ice axe,** which developed from a long pole called an alpenstock, is by far the single most important piece of snow climbing equipment. It becomes virtually an extra limb; it ensures safety and with it a person may travel across otherwise impassable snowy or icy terrain. The trouble, of course, is that, like everthing else these days, ice axes have become specialized and what is good for one particular type of climb may be bad for another. The traditional axe is quite long in the shaft so that when held by the head, the point is touching the ground. The head has a thin, pointed pick at one end for cutting hard ice and a broad adze at the other for cutting snow. The bottom of the axe terminates in a steel spike or ferrule. The long shaft makes it suitable for prodding snow to test snow

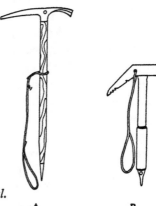

28 *Ice axes: A General purpose or traditional.*
B Short axe for steep ice climbing   **A**   **B**

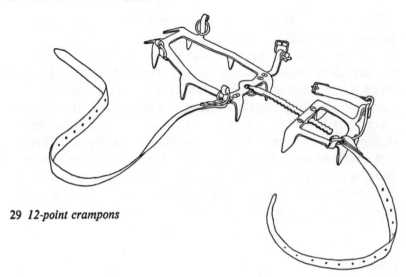

29 *12-point crampons*

bridges over crevasses and for reaching down to cut steps below you when descending. The shaft can be made of hickory, ash, metal or fibreglass and has a sliding wrist sling.

If climbers have a very steep climb in mind they will probably prefer a short-shafted axe or even a **hammer-axe**. These are handier for cutting steps up very steep snow and ice and their disadvantage in downhill cutting or crevasse prodding is knowingly accepted. People become very attached to their ice axes, companions of many an epic climb. It is important to choose an axe not only to suit the type of climbing you have in mind but also one which feels good in your hand. This is a question of the balance of the axe. It should be well weighted in the head and should swing nicely. For the very steepest climbing a pair of short axes with down-curving picks are used.

Crampons come next in importance. They are made of metal, are strapped to the boots, and have ten or twelve sharp points which bite into hard snow or ice enabling the mountaineer to walk easily where he would otherwise be slithering all over the place or having to delay by cutting steps with his ice axe. There are four points on the heel section of the crampons and six downward points on the ball of the foot. Climbers who plan to climb steep routes will certainly choose a twelve-point pair of crampons, the final two points facing forward from the toes. Then, on a steep slope, the foot is kicked straight in and the two forward points bite into the snow or ice. This is called 'front pointing' and is the key to hard snow and ice climbing. Crampons should fit tightly to the boots. A sloppy fit is both disconcerting and dangerous. Many people buy adjustable crampons so that they can be fitted to successive pairs of climbing boots which may vary slightly in size and shape.

Security is a problem on snow and ice, more particularly on soft snow. On ice or hard snow **ice pitons** may be inserted for use as No 2's belay point, for a running belay for the leader or even for climbing steep ice by artificial methods using tape ladders. Among the best ice pitons are the 'Wort Hogs.' This is a metal spike with a coarse outside thread which is hammered directly in but has to be screwed out. Less effective or convenient types include tubular screws which cut out a core of ice, corkscrew types and enlarged versions of blade or channel rock pitons. A belay in soft snow can best be obtained with a **deadman**, a metal plate which is buried deep and so angled that it should be forced even deeper on shock loading. If glacier crossing is involved, with the hazard of falling into a crevasse, then **prusik slings** are needed. They are loops of cord, made of Italian hemp or nylon, which are tied round the climbing rope with a special prusik knot. They can then be used to climb up a rope and out of a crevasse by a special technique, to be described later. In fact they are a light and cheap alternative to ascenders, if less convenient.

The extra clothing needed for snow work includes a pair of nylon or canvas **snow gaiters** which tie under the instep of the boot, hook into the bootlace and come up to the top of the calf. These are useful in keeping the feet and legs dry because there is nothing more wetting than trudging through soggy snow. Remember also that the intensity of the sun is much increased both at high altitude and by radiation off the snow. **Snow goggles** and **sun cream** are necessary.

Snow and Ice Climbing Technique

Step cutting with an ice axe is a craft of which the professional alpine guide is the undisputed master. It is a joy to watch one at work, cutting in two or three easy, well-swung blows a beautifully fashioned step which it takes the amateur a dozen chops to equal. Step cutting should first be practised on a steep snow bank with a harmless snow run-out below.

Big snow slopes are best climbed in a series of zig-zag traverses across the slope. One of the first things to take into account when step cutting is whether you might want to come down the same way, using the same steps. A longish step is quite easy on the ascent but very awkward on the descent. If descent by the same route is contemplated, cut the steps close together. As in rock climbing, balance is important. Resist the temptation to lean in, which only makes your footing less secure; stand upright in the steps. On an upward zig-zag, the step for the lower foot is first cut, forward and about on a level with the present upper foot. Having completed that, the next step for the upper foot is also cut, above and a little forward of the step cut for the lower foot. Both feet are then moved forward to the two new steps, and so on.

Cutting straight up a slope is simply done by cutting a pair of steps at a session and stepping up onto them. If the snow or ice is very steep, hand-holds may be cut. This is done with the adze in snow and with the pick in ice.

When No 2 moves across steps already cut, the axe is either plunged in to the head in soft snow or held across the body, ferrule into the snow on easy ground or with the pick pressed into the slope on steeper ground.

Snow conditions can vary widely, causing the climber to adjust his technique accordingly. For instance, a slope might have been climbed in the morning on wonderfully hard, crisp snow when it was enough to cut a nick with one swing of the axe. This is quite firm enough to support the weight of the climber with just the edge of his boot in the nick, rather as if it were on a nice, small rock hold. In the afternoon, when the slope is being descended, the sun may have been playing on it so that the

30 *Step cutting on a snow traverse*

31 *Snow belay using an ice axe*

climbers sink in above their knees and come wallowing down. What had been a safe slope might now be a dangerously unstable one.

Belaying on snow and ice is a very real problem and is seldom so safe and positive as it is on rock. On ice or snow-ice, the best belay point is an ice piton. On firm snow the ice axe should be driven in to the head, upslope of the belayer. He then ties on to the shaft of the axe, the most convenient method being by a figure-of-eight knot in the climbing rope. He should be standing in enlarged steps. The weak point in this belay will be the snow and it is unfortunately easy for the shaft to crumble the snow under shock loading. Also, a wooden shaft is prone to fracture which makes a metal or fiberglass shaft preferable. In soft snow, the strongest belay is attained by burying the axe as deeply as possible sideways to the slope and tying on to the center of the shaft. It is also marginally more secure to sit than to stand. Better still in these conditions is the use of a deadman, the metal plate of which is buried above the belayer. If the snow is suitable and if the plate is inserted at the correct angle, shock loading will bury the plate deeper. However, on really fluffy snow no belay is perfect and extra care must be taken.

In the event of a fall on the average snow slope, the ice axe can be used as an effective and total brake. On very steep or hard snow it can be used as a partial brake which will considerably reduce the shock on the belayer. It is not really effective in a fall on ice but in these circumstances it is to be hoped that the belayer is using one or more good, strong ice pitons.

The instant a climber feels himself falling he should roll onto his face, move his right hand to the head of the axe, his left to the bottom end of the shaft, and press the adze hard into the surface. If the snow is very hard the pick, rather than the adze, is pressed in. This cuts a groove in the snow and acts as a brake that is sufficient to arrest a fall on an easy slope. However, on a steep slope if the body is allowed to remain flat against the snow the smooth clothing acts rather like a toboggan, reduces drag and causes the falling climber to accelerate. To increase friction the body is lifted clear from the surface by bending at the thighs and pressing the knees into the snow. If the snow is very hard the crampons may snag and flip the falling climber into a somersault with consequent complete loss of control. The feet should therefore be lifted clear of hard snow. In the final position the body is held clear on three points: the right hand and forearm holding the axe and the two knees. The left hand is near the left hip, holding the end of the axe, levering the head into the snow. All this may sound rather a lot to think about in the flurry of a fall but in fact it is quite simple. It should be practised thoroughly whereupon it will become second nature in the event of the real thing.

It is also fun as well as being useful to know how to *glissade*, which is really a controlled slide. It should only be carried out when snow conditions are suitable and no ice is present, when there are no crevasses and where there is no lethal drop below. It can be done roped but it is most

32   *Use of a deadman belay. In practice, the deadman should be about 10 feet above the climber.*

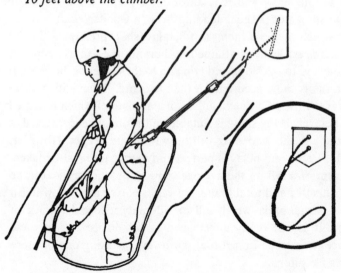

33 *Ice axe used to arrest a fall*

enjoyable where a snow slope eases out at the bottom and the party can safely unrope. To glissade the feet are flattened onto the slope, toes downhill. The left hand grasps the head of the axe, the right holds the ferrule against the snow. As the climber slides the brake is applied by pressing the ferrule into the snow. If the feet will not slide, a sitting glissade may be tried but it will wet the seat of the trousers.

Having learned how to use the ice axe, the time has arrived to put crampons on. They instantly make a world of difference. The climber can walk across smooth ice, the points crunching in to give a sure grip. He can walk up snow slopes where he would otherwise be laboriously cutting steps. One word of caution about cramponing: if the snow becomes wet and tacky, especially in the afternoon sun, the crampons will 'ball up'. Large snowballs collect under the foot and this is very slippery. When this begins to happen, crampons should be taken off.

On a traverse, the foot is placed sideways, with the ankle bent over, to give all the points on the sole a grip on the snow or ice. It is on a direct ascent of a steep slope that crampons really come into their own. It is, however, a great advantage if the soles of the boots are stiffened if they are to be used for front-pointing straight up a climb. In other words a flexible hill-walking boot is unsuitable. With stiff soles the climber can then walk straight up a formidably steep slope. This can be taken to extremes when the climber uses a short axe in each hand and front-points up a near-vertical wall. It puts a massive strain on the calf muscles. Two things are vital: first that the climber should be super-fit and second that there are easements in the ice wall where rests and belays are possible. However, this technique has enabled ice climbs of the hardest grade to be climbed with a rapidity unthinkable had traditional step cutting methods been used.

Because snow conditions can vary so widely and consequently transform the difficulty of a climb, snow and ice climbs are not graded in North America.

Crevasse Rescue

Because glaciers are slowly moving rivers of ice they are, like ordinary rivers, subject to turbulence when they flow steeply downhill or pass over

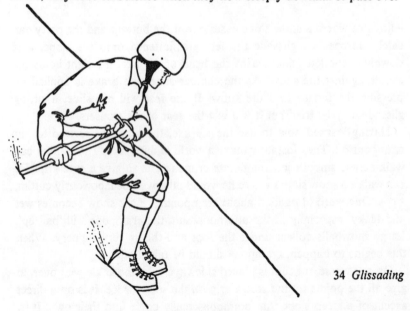

34 *Glissading*

major obstructions. In a river this shows as broken water. On a glacier the result is an icefall or bands of crevasses. Icefalls are areas of chaotic ice strewn with tottering blocks, some as big as a house called *seracs*. They are best avoided. Crevasses are deep splits in the ice, some as deep as 120 ft. The winter snow covers these crevasses with a snow bridge which is always thinner in the centre and may be fragile. Sometimes a crevasse bridge is difficult to spot and can only be detected by a slight depression in the snow. In the summer the snow melts at lower altitudes exposing the ice of the glaciers and the crevasses become obvious chasms in the ice. Higher up the mountain they will remain bridged all the year round by snow of varying quality. Snow bridges which may be as hard as iron in the freezing temperatures of the early morning may be soggy, crumbly and dangerous in the heat of the day.

Mountaineering often involves crossing or climbing sections of glacier. Crevasse negotiation is therefore a necessary skill. When one is spotted No 2 secures the leader with an ice axe belay. The leader advances cautiously, prodding the snow with his ice axe—and this is where a long shaft pays off. If his axe meets firm resistance all is well. If it breaks through into fresh air all is *not* well! He is standing on a dangerously thin snow bridge. It is then best to try an alternative line and find a place where the crevasse is more strongly bridged.

It is possible to fall into a crevasse through inattention, bad judgement or just bad luck. In fact most mountaineers will have broken through a good few snow bridges in their time but usually only the front leg breaks through or at the worst they go down no further than their armpits.

If a party is caught unawares a man may not only break through a crevasse bridge but he may fall a considerable distance and injure himself seriously. It will then need a stretcher and the manpower of a rescue team to get him out. However, what more usually happens is that a climber

35 *Prusik knot*

36 *Self-rescue from a crevasse using three Prusik slings*

breaks through a bridge and falls a relatively short distance before his No 2 is able to arrest the fall. The party should then be able to extricate the fallen man using its own resources.

Before he sets foot on a glacier a mountaineer will tie two or three prusik slings onto the climbing rope close to his waist using a prusik knot. This knot can be pushed up the rope but tightens when weight is

37   *Bilgheri method of crevasse rescue*

put on the prusik sling, for instance by a man standing in it. Ascenders are more convenient to use than prusik slings but their weight is significant. Many climbers find themselves carrying more than enough already without burdening themselves with heavy ascenders for which lightweight prusik slings are an acceptable alternative.

When a climber falls into a crevasse and finds himself dangling between the smooth, icy walls, the first thing he does is unravel the prusik slings. If he has three he will place one foot in each of the longer slings and put the shorter one behind his shoulders to help him keep upright without having to pull with his arms. If he is wearing a thigh harness he will need two slings only: one tied to his harness and the other for one of his feet. At the top all No 2 has to do is hold the rope tight round the ice axe belay. This is quite easy if the snow is firm but it can be a hard tussle in crumbly snow. The man down the crevasse works his way up the rope, pushing first one sling then the other up the rope and stepping up in turn. After a little upward progress has been made it is a good idea for him to take off his rucksack and clip it with a carabiner into the loop of the climbing rope now hanging below. Not only is the climber freed of an encumbrance but the weight of the rucksack keeps the rope taut and makes it easier to move the prusik knots. Eventually he will be able to struggle over the lip of the crevasse back to the surface. The whole operation is very tiring and it is advisable to practice it in an open crevasse to become familiar with the sequence of movements and to appreciate the effort required.

Because of the crevasse danger, a party of two is at some risk on a glacier and a party of three or more is safer. With three an improved method of rescue is possible. No 2 holds fast on the belay while No 3 goes forward to the crevasse and drops down a spare rope (or the other end of the climbing rope) with a loop, or better a webbing ladder, tied in it. There are now two ropes going down to the leader. He is extracted by the 'Bilgheri' method. He puts a foot in the loop and stands up or climbs the rungs of the ladder. The other rope is then taken in until it becomes tight round his waist. The loop or ladder is then pulled up a foot or so for him to step up again. This is quicker and easier than the method first described. One important point is to agree on the method to be used *before* you go onto the glacier so that if a mishap happens, everyone knows what is to be done.

Avalanches

Where there is snow on a mountainside there is an avalanche hazard and this is a major cause of mountain accidents. Sometimes the danger is obvious, such as after a heavy snowfall when it is clear that the loose snow will slide down the mountainside. As a general rule it is unwise, as well as being very laborious, to climb immediately after a heavy snowfall.

Common sense will help you avoid most dangers. If you can see the scars down the snowslopes caused by avalanches, with their characteristic lobes at the bottom, or if you can see and hear avalanches in the area, then the danger is obvious. If you get onto a snow slope and the snow feels slithery and unstable, then let your instinct be your guide and get off the snow if it feels unsafe. Be particularly vigilant if there is a sudden rise in temperature because this can permit a slope to avalanche which, until then, was held by the action of frost. Also, convex slopes are more potentially dangerous than concave ones.

The subject of snow structure and avalanches is, however, very complicated and there are no simple and safe rules. Much depends on the friction between layers of snow below the surface and this is often quite unpredictable by the mountaineer. Experience and caution are necessary—and you can still be caught out.

Ice avalanches are more predictable. It is unwise to travel below an icefall because the tottering seracs are in constant slow movement and sooner or later must come crashing down. Similarly, in late spring the overhanging lips of snow along the ridges, called *cornices*, are liable to break and fall. Try to avoid climbing beneath them especially in periods of warm weather. It is also important when climbing along a ridge not to go too close to the edge until you have confirmed that it is not corniced, or you may break through. Climbers always keep well below the crest line on a corniced ridge.

Chapter 8

Survival and Rescue

With mournful regularity we hear news reports of 'party overwhelmed by blizzard' or 'mountaineer dies of exposure'. The sad thing is that, when the full story comes out, it often transpires that the disaster was avoidable. Too often a party is caught with inadequate equipment or gets into worse trouble than it need by making a faulty decision. It is, I admit, easy to criticize, but the fact remains that there are recognized rules about warm clothing that should be worn but is not, about items of safety equipment that should be carried but are left behind. There is sound guidance about what it is best to do if overtaken by foul weather or night, or both, but this is sometimes ignored in the stress of an emergency.

Two points are of paramount importance when something goes dangerously wrong. The first and probably the most difficult thing is to acknowledge instantly that you are in a survival situation and nothing else matters. Your priorities in life must be radically altered and this requires a very positive mental effort, possibly in distressing circumstances. Next, the mind will react strongly against the present uncomfortable and dangerous situation. You crave for the emergency to end and to get back to comfortable normalcy. There is a powerful temptation to go for easy options, to think, 'If only we can just do so-and-so all will come right'. It won't. One of the most valuable things I have learnt on my many expeditions to the polar regions and to the high mountains is that, when things go wrong, the hard option is the right decision. Take a tough line, and take it early, and you will greatly increase your chances of survival.

Spending a night out in the mountains, in other words bivouacking, is not necessarily unpleasant. In the big ranges some routes are so long that they cannot be completed in a single day, making a *planned bivouac* necessary. Food and lightweight cooking utensils are carried. Usually the climbers will have a down jacket which they might augment either with a sleeping bag or half a sleeping bag, called a *pied d'elephant*, to cover their lower limbs. In case it rains during the night it is wise to carry some waterproof covering in the form of a polythene or light nylon bag. In favourable conditions a planned bivouac can be positively enjoyable.

A *forced bivouac*, where the climbers are overtaken and immobilized by darkness or bad weather, is a very different matter. Mountaineers cannot always climb loaded down with bivouac gear. There is a saying that if you go fully prepared for a bivouac, then you are bound to have one. A forced bivouac will therefore be both cold and makeshift. There will be no hot food. However, climbers on a high mountain should be carrying down jackets and a cagoule and waterproof trousers. This should keep them dry and protect them against the worst bite of the cold, although they will spend a shivery night. Extra protection can be gained by putting the legs into the rucksack and by huddling together. In this sort of situation there are really no choices open. If darkness or bad weather makes it impossible to climb up or down, then you have got to stay put. A forced bivouac, except in a long-drawn-out storm, is nothing to worry about and happens to most mountaineers in their time.

Exposure or Mountain Hypothermia

A group caught by storm in easier mountain country, hill walking for instance, can be faced with a more difficult choice. If the terrain is not unduly difficult, it maybe possible to continue to move despite the conditions. This is where it is possible to make a fatal error, especially if visibility has become bad, the group is getting tired and is not sure of its position. The leader of a youth group might be so appalled at the prospect of his young party facing the hazard of a night out in a blizzard that he will force on towards what he assumes to be, but does not positively know, is a point of safety. If his hunch pays off, all is well and we hear nothing of it. If his 'point of safety' is not attained then some of the weaker members may easily die of exposure as a direct result of his over-optimistic decision-making. In other words he took the attractive, soft option because he could not bring himself to take the hard decision.

True, the cold will kill but it will only do so slowly over a period of days if the victim starts well clothed and dry, well fed and reasonably fresh. Exposure, or mountain hypothermia to give it its correct name, can kill a physically and mentally exhausted man in a matter of hours. Teenagers are more likely to succumb to exhaustion than adults. To make things more dangerous, the symptoms of exposure are difficult to recognize. There is no space to deal with the whole subject of first aid but as exposure is a very specific mountain hazard, I will go into some detail.

The wet, aggravated by the wind, is the real killer. Let us compare two people who are benighted. A seasoned mountaineer who has kept himself dry, has spare clothing, a completely waterproof covering in the form of a cagoule and waterproof trousers, and a good supply of spare food in his rucksack will survive the roughest of nights in the mountains and walk home the next morning, a little battered by the elements perhaps, but not much the worse for his experience.

By contrast, an inexperienced teenager goes out for a day's hill walking but finds the distance too much for him and gets very tired. It was a warm day when he started so he was wearing his favourite jeans, a light pullover and an old windproof that was not waterproof. He ate all his food at lunchtime. In the evening, he was getting towards the end of his tether. Then cloud came down, reducing the visibility to nil and it began to pour with rain. He was well and truly stuck. Soon he was wet to the skin and began to shiver. Finally a biting wind came up which seemed to suck the warmth out of his very bones, even though the temperature was not even freezing. In other words the heat loss from his wet, exhausted, unfed body was immense. His chances of surviving the night would be slim and by morning he would probably be dead of mountain hypothermia.

The word 'exposure' is often used loosely, so let us start by defining it more precisely. The inner core (trunk and brain) of the body must remain at a constant 37°C (98.6°F) even though the outer shell may become much cooler. If the inner core temperature falls, hypothermia results, which leads to mental deterioration and loss of muscle co-ordination and eventually to unconsciousness, heart and respiratory failure and death. *The vital thing to remember is that any treatment given must maintain or increase the inner core temperature.* Anything that merely stimulates the peripheral circulation will send warm blood to the surface, where it will rapidly cool and then reduce the core temperature on its return to the heart. The result could be fatal.

In foul weather everyone feels cold and miserable and suffers to some degree from exposure. When communication is difficult anyway it may not be at all easy to identify the point when a member of the party has reached the stage when he has in effect become a casualty. Indeed a person may be walking reasonably strongly and three hours later be dead from mountain hypothermia.

Because a victim of exposure becomes muddled, he is seldom able either to recognize his predicament or to do much to help himself although he may complain of the cold generally or cramp in the legs. The main responsibility therefore falls on the leader who must be on the alert for any of the following symptoms:

1. *Inconspicuousness*—quietness, apathy, lack of enthusiasm, slowing pace, a pale face nearly always near the end of the line.
2. *Slow thinking*—does not answer questions or refer to map when asked; cannot perform tasks well within his level of skill and knowledge; does not react to commands; forgets or ignores things such as gloves, loose bootlaces; careless footwork on broken ground.
3. *Unexpected behaviour*—he may do quite unreasonable things, physically resist help, use violent language or exhibit sudden outbursts of energy.
4. *Loss of faculties*—the speech may be slurred, vision disturbed, muscle co-ordination may fail causing stumbling and falling.
5. *Shivering*—in violent fits.
6. *Loss of consciousness*—this is a late and grave sign.

Prevention is always better than cure and an experienced leader will get his party down to safety before conditions so deteriorate as to make mountain hypothermia a danger. However, miscalculations do occur and if a party begins to get tired while still a good way from home, and if there is a real doubt that shelter and safety may be reached, then the correct action is to halt the party and get them out of the wind. It could be fatal to force on. A protective boulder might be found, a windbreak may be built of stones. In an open snowfield, it is necessary to dig a hole which may vary from a simple trench to a snow cave. All spare clothing should be put on and emergency rations eaten.

If it is confirmed or even suspected that a member of the party is suffering from exposure, he should be placed in a sleeping bag in a slightly head-down position in the most sheltered place available and fit members of the party should lie beside him to warm him up. If available, hot drinks should be given and the casualty should be encouraged to take any easily digested food, especially sugary things. NEVER give him alcohol. Neither should he be given a hot water bottle or be rubbed to stimulate circulation. If he stops breathing give mouth-to-mouth ('kiss of life') artificial respiration until the patient breathes normally or until a doctor arrives and tells you to stop. The casualty must be carried down by stretcher even if he says he is feeling better and able to walk.

These notes are necessarily abbreviated. It is strongly recommended that a fuller account of the causes and treatment of exposure should be studied. There is an excellent book published by the Mountaineers of Seattle entitled *Medicine for Mountaineering* which treats this subject, and others.

Accident Procedure

If an accident occurs it may be possible to summon immediate help from other climbers or hill walkers in the vicinity. For this purpose there is a recognized alpine distress signal which consists of six blasts on the whistle or six light flashes repeated at minute intervals. A red flare has the same meaning. The reply is three whistle blasts or three flashes repeated at minute intervals or a white flare.

If an accident occurs the first thing to do is to ensure that the party is secured so as to prevent a second and possibly worse accident happening. The casualty is, of course, given first aid and made as warm and comfortable as possible. If no one answers the distress signal self-help is called for. In the ideal party of four, one member stays with the casualty while the other two climb or walk down for help. If there are three in the party and the descent is not too hazardous, one man always remains with the casualty. In a party of two there is, of course, no choice and the casualty must be left unattended while his companion summons help.

If the injury is such that the casualty is obviously a stretcher case additional manpower will be necessary to get him off the mountain. Before setting out, the leader, or preferably the whole party, should have noted where the nearest rescue post is. This post, which is sometimes marked on the map, is usually a house in the valley and will have rescue equipment, including a stretcher, and some means of communication to alert the rescue team. If the casualty is not too seriously injured and is in an accessible position, it may be possible to enlist some local helpers and carry him back in the stretcher wihout too much fuss.

On the other hand if the casualty is either seriously injured or is in an inaccessible position, half-way up a climb for instance, then it is necessary to call out a mountain rescue team. These teams exist in many climbing areas and are usually composed of local climbers who voluntarily give their time, and often take great risks, to bring help to their fellow mountaineers in distress. They often dig deep into their own pockets to purchase and maintain their special equipment which includes mountain stretchers, elaborate lowering apparatus, powerful lights and radios. It is usual to telephone the police, and not the rescue team, in the first instance. The police have the authority to call out the rescue team or to request air evacuation by helicopter if this appears quicker and more suitable. They can also order an ambulance to stand by.

A rescue team needs, above all, accurate information. If the accident happened on a named climbing route, the name of the crag, the route, and the exact pitch on the route where the casualty is lying should be given to the rescue team. With their expert local knowledge they will know the best way of setting about the rescue and whether it would be better, for instance, to raise the casualty or lower him.

If the accident happens in open country more care is needed. This is where a paper and pencil carried in the flap of the rucksack can be so useful. If a map reference can be worked out and jotted down, this is most valuable. It may be possible to take a bearing, or better two, on recognizable features and note them down. At the scene of the accident the casualty may be tucked away behind a rock out of the wind and therefore invisible from below. The spot should be marked by placing a bright object, such as a coloured rucksack in a prominent position. If rope is available it can be strung out to its full length which can be effective in very bad visibility. At night a light should be shone.

If a team is called out to rescue you, write them a letter of appreciation and, if you can afford it, send a donation to the rescue team funds. It is a sad reflection on human ingratitude how seldom a rescued victim takes the trouble even to say thank you.

Mountain accidents are frequently both reported inaccurately and sensationalized by the media. This is not only irritating but it often portrays mountaineering in an unfair and unfavourable light. It is therefore important to avoid making unconsidered statements to the media, perhaps while still under the mental and physical stress of the accident. If a reporter appears on the scene of an accident, refer him to the mountaineer who is in overall charge of the rescue.

Chapter 9

Try It!

Having got so far let us assume that you have decided to give mountaineering a try. What have you let yourself in for?

First, it is an activity that will last you all your life, unlike the more hectic field games. In fact quite recently I enjoyed a delightful climb with a retired admiral in his seventy-ninth year! If you take up climbing you will certainly have some tough times when you are cold, frightened or weary, sometimes all at the same time, but in sharing these trials with like-minded companions you will develop deep and long-lasting friendships, not casually made, but tested in hardship. And the wise man knows the true value of friends in life.

Mountaineering is a pursuit which can, and often does, exert an absorbing, even dominating, influence over your life. It occupies many or most weekends and culminates in the mountaineering holiday. This may take place in the homeland hills or abroad but always new scenes, new people and new interests are discovered.

Climbing high mountains is a great and wonderful endeavour, to be compared with ocean sailing in a small boat or crossing deserts or ice caps. It tests and extends a man or woman to the full limit of mental and physical ability and sometimes, it seems, even beyond that limit. The reward, in terms of challenge and fulfilment, and in the transcending splendour of the mountain scene, is beyond price.

Have a go—but carefully!

*   *   *   *

Appendix

Where to Climb in the United States and Canada

by Andy Kauffman

The United States and Canada are big countries with lots of places to climb and many kinds of climbing. Here follows a short sketch of the most important.

There is no general register of North American climbing regions. Accordingly, the climber must seek information from a number of local and regional guidebooks of varying standards and quality, or from climbing organizations. And while there are many excellent professional individual leaders and teachers, mountain guides and climbing schools are not required to meet any criteria. Because the novice often lacks the ability to distinguish between good and poor service, almost all should be approached with caution.

By contrast the major national and regional climbing clubs can provide competence and knowledgeability; their managements feel a responsibility to the public. Those clubs listed below are therefore the best sources of assistance for the beginner who is looking for good teachers and places to climb.

In the United States the national organization of mountaineering is the *American Alpine Club* (AAC), 113 East 90th Street, New York, New York, 10028, telephone (212) 722-1628. While membership is restricted to experienced climbers with a continuing interest in the sport, the club nevertheless has a responsibility as a tax-free foundation to serve public needs. Thus it will usually answer general inquiries promptly and courteously. The club's wealth of information on American mountaineering is unmatched, but it does not seek to supply detailed information in the areas served by the various regional organizations.

The *Alpine Club of Canada* (ACC) is that country's national climbing organization. Its headquarters are P.O. Box 1026, Banff, Alberta, Canada, TOLOCO, telephone (403) 762-3664.

There are a few regional clubs in Canada of which the most noteworthy are, in the East, the *Fédération Québecoise de la Montagne,* 1415 Jassy Street East, Montreal, P.Q., Canada, telephone (514) 374-4700 and, in the West, the *Mountaineering Club of British Columbia,* P.O. Box 2674, Vancouver, British Columbia, Canada, telephone not listed.

The hill country of the United States consists of three regions: 1) east of the Rocky Mountains, where suitable areas are scarce, but which are important because of their location near population centers; 2) the area from the Rocky Mountains to the Pacific, where one finds most of the best mountains within the contiguous forty-eight states; and, 3) Alaska, which has the country's highest and most important ranges. Mountaineering in the East is restricted almost exclusively to rock-work, while in the West, especi lly in Washington and Oregon, one finds considerable ice and snow. Alaskan climbing is chiefly expeditionary in nature.

The principal eastern and central climbing areas can be conveniently subdivided:

1) **New England and New York:**

a) *Maine,* with two important sites: *Acadia National Park* on Mount Desert Island where granite cliffs rise several hundred feet from the ocean. This is a gentle region of alternating blue skies and mists and is best visited in summer. The climbing guide may now be out of print, but, if not, it should be obtainable from the Appalachian Mountain Club in Boston. Mile-high *Mount Katahdin,* situated in isolated and grandiose Baxter State Park northwest of Millinocket, is the state's other chief climbing area. Most routes are long. The area is subject to violent, sudden storms, even in summer. No climbing guidebooks are currently available.

b) *New Hampshire* has some of the best rock-climbing east of the Mississippi. There are two principal areas: first, the Mount Washington Valley from Conway north along State Route 16. *Mount Washington,* at the north end of the area, rises to almost 6,300 feet and has good continuous climbing above timberline in its Huntington Ravine, as well as excellent winter and spring ice-climbing. Weather conditions are among the most severe in North America, especially in winter. Just west of North Conway are 600-foot granite *Cathedral* and *White Horse* Ledges with numerous itineraries. Those on Cathedral are uniformly severe, while those on White Horse are less so. A guidebook, *A Climber's Guide to the Mount Washington Valley* by Cote, published in a limited edition, may still be available from the Appalachian Mountain Club or from Eastern Mountain Sports in North Conway. The second area is *Cannon Mountain,* outside Franconia, with its lengthy, spectacular 800-foot cliff, which rises directly above U.S. Route 3. Climbs are long, varied, require skill and in some places the granite is unstable. There is a guidebook of average quality, *Cannon Cliff,* by Peterson and Porter, White Owls Production, Box 575, South Lancaster, Massachusetts.

c) *New York* also offers two principal areas, plus a number of relatively untouched outcrops. In the northeast, west of I-87 near Plattsburg, are the granite cliffs of the *Adirondacks* with a network of 300–700-foot cliffs. Routes vary in difficulty, but many are severe. A comprehensive guidebook, *A Climber's Guide to the Adirondacks* by Healy, published by the Adirondack Mountain Club, 1971, is available. There also exist other guidebooks to the area. Seventy miles north of New York City, just west of New Paltz off I-87, lie the quartzite *Shawangunks,* the most extensive rock-climbing area in the East and also, because of the quality of the rock and proximity to the nation's largest metropolitan center, the most developed. The cliffs lie mostly on the property of the Mohonk Trust which charges a nominal users' fee. They extend several miles and offer a multitude of routes of from 75 feet to 200 feet, of every level of difficulty. This is probably the best place in the East to acquire technical rock skill. The guidebook, *Shawangunk Rock Climbs* by Williams, published in 1972 by the American Alpine Club, is the best of its kind in existence, complete with almost 400 graded route descriptions and photographs of each. An important area, though crowded on weekends.

2) **West Virginia,** the next area of importance, has its chief climbing near the Germany Valley just east of U.S. 33 at its intersection with State Routes 4 and 28. Principal climbs are found on *Champe, Seneca* and *Nelson* Rocks and rise from 200 to 500 feet above their bases. Seneca, which served as a training ground for mountain troops in World War II, is by far the most frequented. Rock is also a quartzite of reasonably good quality which forms attractive pinnacles reminiscent of alpine summits of difficult access. The rural countryside is of great beauty, but the rock becomes intolerably hot in summer, so it is best to

visit this country in spring and autumn. There is an adequate *Climber's Guide to Seneca Rocks, West Virginia* by Robinson, published 1971 by the Mountaineering Section of the Potomac Appalachian Trail Club. It contains eighty route descriptions and some good sketches.

3) **North Carolina,** somewhat neglected, has much of the East's best climbing. The two principal areas are *Table Rock-Linville Gorge* and the forbidding *granite domes* farther south. Linville Gorge and its neighbor, Table Rock, are situated near Morgantown in the heart of the southern rhododendron forest. Table Rock, visible from a distance, has numerous routes of every degree and grade on an extended 300-foot face. Linville Gorge, not easily seen, offers 300–600 foot metamorphic cliffs that extend for several miles along the valley. Around Cashiers on the eastern flank of the Blue Ridge are Carolina's principal granite domes. Some are extremely impressive with faces of 800 feet to 1,100 feet. Rock here is exceptionally firm and most climbing is on slabs with few good belay points. Climbing is often extremely severe, once committed retreat can be difficult, and the area is therefore recommended for experienced persons. Carolina areas are best visited in the cool months. *The Carolina Climber's Guide* by Buddy Price, published privately, gives a detailed outline of location and grades of most Carolina climbing areas. It may be obtained by writing the author at Route 6, P.O. Box 554, Piedmont, North Carolina.

4) **Wisconsin** has some good climbing in the vicinity of *Devil's Lake* and a few lesser sites. The area is mentioned because it has a number of 100-foot pinnacles which represent almost the only significant climbing in a radius of several hundred miles.

5) **South Dakota** is the only other major climbing area east of the Rocky Mountains. The climbs are situated in Custer State Park in the *Black Hills* where a constellation of pegmatite pinnacles, some 400 to 600 feet high, rise out of the surrounding countryside. The rock is firm but safety points are sometimes scarce or at best precarious. Despite occasional hot afternoons, the region is at its best in summer. The guidebook, *A Climber's Guide to the Needles of South Dakota* by Kamps, published in 1971 by the American Alpine Club, is the most recent and complete available.

By far the most important climbing in the contiguous forty-eight states is in the western third of the country, where mountains are generally high. Much of it requires skill in camping, rock-climbing, snow-and-ice craft and general knowledge of mountain travel. Generally speaking the snow-covered alpine sites lie in the Pacific Northwest, while rock is predominant in the Southwest. The best known areas are:

1) **Wyoming,** with two major mountain chains. The granitic, accessible *Tetons* in Grand Teton National Park just south of the Yellowstone rise to over 13,000 feet above small glaciers. Here is some of the finest rock-climbing in the country and also a modicum of ice and snow. Near Jackson Hole the American Alpine Club maintains a Climber's Ranch where the public may stay for a nominal fee. The classic guidebook, *A Climber's Guide to the Teton Range* by Ortenburger, published 1962 by the Sierra Club, is excellent, but now somewhat out of date. A revised edition is believed to be in preparation. South of the Tetons, the *Wind River Range,* of approximately equal altitude, has excellent rock climbs, but requires a one- to two-day approach march through remote and esthetic country. The best guidebook is the *Field Book to the Wind Rivers* by Bonney, published privately in 1968. Also in Wyoming's southeast, in limbo between the Rockies and Black Hills, is *Devil's Tower,* an isolated volcanic plug whose cliffs rise 800 feet and more on all sides. No known guidebooks exist, but visitors may consult photographic route descriptions available on Devil Tower National Monument grounds.

2) **Colorado,** the Union's highest state, is also the site of most of its tallest summits (14,000 feet +) outside Alaska. The most popular groups from a climbing standpoint are the *Frontal Ranges* in Rocky Mountain National Park northwest of Denver where fine, lengthy rock faces may be scaled on *Long's Peak* and others. Outside Boulder is a frequented practice area, the *Flatirons.* Other areas include, in the south-center, *Gunnison River Canyon* with its 2,000 foot walls and, in the southwest, the less well known *Needle Mountains* of the San Juans in the Telluride-Durango region. Most ascents everywhere require approach marches and bivouacs. There are no major glaciers in the state, but occasional névés provide a chance to practice snow craft even in summer. The most comprehensive guidebook is the *Guide to the Colorado Mountains* by Ormes, 1970 edition published by Sage Books under the auspices of the Colorado Mountain Club. It provides detailed coverage of all areas.

3) **New Mexico** has several good climbing spots, the principal being the *Sandia* mountains east of Albuquerque with extensive faces of

1,500 to 2,000 feet of all levels of difficulty. These are best visited in the cool weather of spring and fall. Also worth mention is desert-surrounded *Shiprock* in northwest New Mexico with its 2,000-foot face. Once a popular climb, it is currently subject to restrictions because it lies on Indian tribal lands. There are no known formal guidebooks to New Mexico climbing.

4) **Montana's** best climbing is around *Granite Peak,* highest point of the little-known *Absoroka* range north of Yellowstone Park, where there are small glaciers and good granite. The area lends itself to exploration as there are no guidebooks. The peaks of *Glacier National Park* ("Glacier," by the way, is almost a misnomer) are not recommended for climbers owing to the rock's poor quality.

5) **Utah** has a large number of climbing areas of which the best known are the *Arches* and the cliffs of *Zion National Park* in the south. Here the sandstone rock varies in soundness, though the *Great White Throne* has several good routes. There are no known guidebooks.

6) **Arizona** has a multitude of possibilities about which there is little published data. Most are mesas and pillars far out in the desert. Many of these are on Indian tribal lands where access is restricted; others, notably in the Grand Canyon, have poor rock. But generally speaking the state, with its stark, haunting beauty, contains as much untouched rock-climbing as its western counterparts combined, and merits exploration by beginners and experts alike. Information on Arizona climbing may be obtained from the Arizona Mountaineering Club, and, peripherally, from the Mountaineering Section of the Sierra Club.

7) **Idaho's** principal climbing district, mostly rock, consists of the *Sawtooth Range* in the southcentral area around Sun Valley. Peaks with excellent faces rise to about 11,000–12,000 feet and are of reasonably easy access through open forest. There is no known guidebook.

8) **Washington** encompasses most of the ice and snow areas of the forty-eight contiguous states. The mountains are mostly situated in the west and have a complex geologic structure. The *Cascades* offer mixed climbing both on rock and ice and snow. They are extensive and sometimes remote of access. Peaks here are of two formations: metamorphic and granitic, and dormant volcanos. Of the former, *Mt. Shuksan* and the mountains of the *Chelan* area are among the best known. Principal volcanos are mounts *Baker, St. Helens* and *Rainier.* This last, over 14,000 feet and situated in the National Park of that

name, has America's best ice and snow outside Alaska. Weather can be formidable. In the extreme west, the *Olympics,* rising to about 8,000-9,000 feet, have some good ice and snow and a few interesting peaks. Much of the region is hard of access owing to location on a peninsula and sometimes difficult approaches through heavy rain forest. There is a fine guidebook to the Cascades and Olympics which, however, some people feel to be overly detailed: *A Climber's Guide to Cascade and Olympic Mountains of Washington* by Beckey, published by the Mountaineers.

9) **Oregon's** principal summits are volcanos, the chief being glaciated *Mount Hood,* over 12,000 feet, east of Portland, the scene of much mountain trekking. Here and there throughout the state are some good cliffs and mountains, but these are by no means as extensive and alpine as Washington's Cascades.

10) **California's** main attraction is the massive granite country of Yosemite National Park which constitutes one of the finest, most accessible and esthetic rock climbing areas in the world. Many of America's best climbers took their first steps here. The granite cliffs vary from 200 to 2,000 feet and more. The rock is remarkably stable. Spring and fall are the best climbing seasons. There exists a comprehensive guidebook, *A Climber's Guide to Yosemite Valley* by Roper, published 1971 by the Sierra Club. Elsewhere in the state there is a profusion of rock-climbing possibilities, notably in the area around Mount Whitney and elsewhere in the *Sierra Nevada Range.* The region is well covered by a guidebook, *The Climber's Guide to the High Sierras* by Roper, published 1976 by the Sierra Club. In southern California granite *Tahquitz Rock,* though not high in relation to Yosemite, is a fine practice area. There is a guidebook to Tahquitz: *A Climber's Guide to Tahquitz and Suicide Rocks* by Witts, published by the American Alpine Club.

The third United States mountain climbing area is **Alaska.** It has the continent's most extensive mountain system and its highest peaks. The principal areas are the lengthy *Coastal Ranges* which form a vast arc from Ketchikan to the Aleutians and which culminate at the fulcrum of the state's panhandle in *Mount St. Elias.* In the interior lies the *Mount McKinley (Denali)* region which rises to over 20,000 feet. Most climbing is of sub-arctic nature and cannot be recommended to beginners nor, for that matter, to persons lacking in camping and snow and ice experience. There are no official guidebooks, but information is available from the American Alpine Club.

As is the case in the United States, **Canada** lacks a national climbing register. There exists, however, a series of excellent guidebooks of uniform standards which describe the better-known areas. Likewise, guide service is considerably more reliable because it is usually possible to retain the assistance of European-licensed professionals who have had rigorous training and who hold certified diplomas issued by their country of origin.

Excluding the arctic islands and the Northwest Territory-Yukon country, which present the same problems as Alaska and are therefore omitted, Canada can be divided into four climbing regions: 1) the rock cliffs of the Laurentians outside Montreal; 2) the Canadian Rockies; 3) the Interior Ranges of British Columbia; and, 4) the Pacific Coastal Ranges.

1) In effect the **Laurentians** are an extension of the Appalachian Highlands which provide the bulk of eastern United States climbing. The cliffs are rarely above 200 feet high and the best are around *Mont Tremblant* and St. Hilaire northwest of Montreal. Information about these areas may be obtained from the Fédération Québecoise de la Montagne.

2) The **Canadian Rockies,** situated along the border of Alberta and British Columbia, are a huge glaciated mountain system of sedimentary rock extending in a southeast to northwesterly direction from the United States border to the subarctic, four of whose summits exceed 12,000 feet. The many ranges are of varying degrees of accessibility through usually open forests. With exceptions the rock is of poor quality, so most climbs are done on ice and snow. All peaks close to transportation and population centers such as Banff and Jasper have been scaled, but adventurers will find many unclimbed summits, some remarkably easy, by back-packing a couple of days into the interior. Best known areas are in contiguous Banff, Yoho, Kootenay, and Jasper National Parks. There is excellent guide service available in Banff from Canadian Mountain Holidays, P.O. Box 1660, Banff, Alberta, TOLOCO, which retains expert Swiss, Austrian and German-born professionals, and from other organizations of varying reliability, but usually qualified. A first class, comprehensive illustrated guidebook, of necessity limited in detail, is available from Alpine Club of Canada headquarters: *A Climber's Guide to the Rocky Mountains of*

Canada by Putnam, Kruczyna, Jones, and Boles, now in two volumes (North of Howse Pass, and South) published jointly by the American Alpine Club and the Alpine Club of Canada in 1973 and 1974 respectively. This work is under constant review and new editions appear periodically.

3) Somewhat less populated and well known, the British Columbia **Interior Ranges** (Cariboos, Monashees, Selkirks, Purcells) flank the Rockies on the west, being separated from them by the Canoe-Columbia-Kootenay trench. Surrounded mostly by deep rain forests and narrow valleys, the peaks rise to about 11,500 feet and are often difficult of access. The geology is complex, but the rock is usually good and the mountains are heavily glaciated. Once timberline is attained these ranges offer some of the most rewarding and enjoyable climbing in Canada. The guidebook, *A Climber's Guide to the Interior Ranges of British Columbia* by Putnam and Kruczyna, 1977 edition, published jointly by the American Alpine Club and the Alpine Club of Canada, is the counterpart to the Rockies' guide and is also in two volumes. One deals with the area north of the Canadian Pacific Railroad, the other with the area south.

Note that both in the Rockies and Interior Ranges the Alpine Club of Canada and other services maintain a number of huts to accommodate climbers and travellers. Membership in the Alpine Club of Canada is desirable if one wishes to use Club huts since some are kept locked and usage fees are higher for outsiders than for members.

In Canada's extreme west are the **Coast Ranges** which form a barrier between British Columbia's interior and the Pacific. This is a vast region of savage beauty, often impenetrable rain forest, and notoriously bad weather. The climactic portion is the *Waddington Pluton* which rises in a series of serrated, heavily glaciated summits of 11,000 to over 13,000 feet reminiscent of the famous Chamonix needles. Climbing here is of an expeditionary nature and requires skill and reliable companions. A fine guidebook, *A Climber's Guide to the Coastal Ranges of British Columbia* by Culbert, with 1969 supplement, has been published by the Alpine Club of Canada. It is accompanied by an excellent sketch map of the Waddington area.

Good sources of regional and local information are:

North-Eastern states: The *Appalachian Mountain Club,* 5 Joy Street, Boston, Massachusetts, 02108, telephone (617) 523-0636.

East Central and Southern states: The *Mountaineering Section of* *the Potomac Appalachian Trail Club,* 1718 N Street, N.W., Washington, D.C., 20036, telephone (evenings only) (202) 638-5306.

Middle West: The two best-managed organizations are the *Chicago Mountaineering Club* and the *Iowa Mountaineers,* with no fixed headquarters. Inquiries for the Chicago group at this time should be addressed to George Pokorny, 739 Forest Avenue, Glen Ellyn, Illinois, 60137, telephone (312) 469-3443, while those for the Iowa Mountaineers should be sent to John Ebert, 30 Prospect Place, Iowa City, Iowa, 52240, telephone (319) 337-7163.

Rocky Mountain states: The *Colorado Mountain Club,* 2530 West Alameda Avenue, Denver, Colorado, 80218, telephone (303) 922-8315.

Idaho and Washington: The *Mountaineers,* 719 Pike Street, Seattle, Washington, 98218, telephone (206) 623-2314.

Oregon: The *Mazamas,* 909 N.W. 19th Street, Portland, Oregon, 97209, telephone (503) 227-2345.

California: The *Mountaineering Section of the Sierra Club,* 530 Bush Street, San Francisco, California, 94108, telephone (415) 981-8634.

Arizona: The *Arizona Mountaineering Club,* P.O. Box 1695, Phoenix, Arizona, 85001, telephone not listed.

Admission to all these clubs is generally open.

Index